Growing

Business Intelligence

An Agile Approach to Leveraging Data and Analytics for Maximum Business Value

Larry Burns

Published by:

2 Lindsley Road
Basking Ridge, NJ 07920 USA

https://www.TechnicsPub.com

Cover design by John Fiorentino
Edited by Lauren McCafferty
Illustrations by Mateusz Wieczorek

ISBN, print ed.   9781634621472
ISBN, Kindle ed.   9781634621489
ISBN, ePub ed.   9781634621496
ISBN, PDF ed.   9781634621502
ISBN, Audio ed.   9781634621519

First Printing 2016

Library of Congress Control Number: 2016950003

To Becky, who would rather see her husband write something that makes money, but who supports all my dreams, profitable or not.

And to John Giles, my colleague, my friend, my mentor, and my soul brother.

Acknowledgements

First and foremost, I would like to acknowledge a deep debt of gratitude to landscaping and gardening expert Ann Lovejoy, whose seminal work on sustainable landscaping, *The Ann Lovejoy Handbook of Northwest Gardening* (Sasquatch Books, Seattle WA, 2003), provides both the metaphorical underpinning and much of the insight that shapes this book's approach to Data Management and Business Intelligence. It is, I think, a tribute to the universality of Ann's ideas and approach that I have been able to apply them to a realm so apparently far removed from her own. I encourage anyone with an interest in natural and sustainable landscaping and gardening to buy and study Ann's book.

I would also like to acknowledge the continual and ongoing help, support, and encouragement of my colleagues in our organization's BI and Data Services and Enterprise Architecture groups, as well as many fine people in our various business divisions across the globe. I couldn't (and wouldn't) do the work that I do without them.

And last (but not least), I would like to thank Steve Hoberman and the wonderful people at Technics Publications for their encouragement and hard work; this book would never have seen the light of day without their efforts. You'll have to judge for yourself whether that's a good thing.

Table of Contents

Introduction

As organizations I've worked for have made their initial descents into the labyrinth that is business intelligence (commonly abbreviated "BI") and analytics, they are—like Theseus of old was—mostly concerned about surviving the experience. The dangerous Minotaur faced by Theseus is an apt analogy for the challenges presented by BI; the Minotaur, you may recall, was half man and half beast. Similarly, the perils and pitfalls of BI are two-faceted: there are both technological and human obstacles to overcome on the road to BI success.

The technological obstacles of BI are well-known. If you wish to get started with BI, you must first face a bewildering jungle of products, platforms, jargon, and acronyms: big data, Hadoop, NoSQL, IoT, data lakes, data virtualization, data visualization, data warehousing, and on. Each one of these is being continually hawked by persuasive vendors and ardent adherents, and they all require significant capital investment. (I could retire tomorrow on the money that any one of these vendors makes from a single customer engagement!)

Less understood are the human obstacles—the defects and shortcomings of human nature that cause us to over-plan, under-estimate, over-assume, and under-envision. Virtually every failed BI project has been torpedoed by human issues, not technological ones.

It is this combination of technological and human risks that makes BI projects more problematic than perhaps any other IT-dependent initiatives. The often massive up-front cost, coupled with a veritable minefield of process and technology pitfalls, is a return on investment (ROI) disaster just waiting to happen.

So the question becomes: how do we enable our organizations to enjoy the often significant benefits of BI and analytics, while at the same time minimizing the cost and risk of failure? In this book, I am not going to try to be prescriptive; I won't tell you exactly how to build your BI environment. Instead, I am going to focus on a few core principles that will enable you to navigate the rocky shoals of BI architecture and arrive at a destination best suited for your particular organization. Some of these core principles include:

- Have an overarching strategy, plan, and roadmap.

- Recognize and leverage your existing technology investments.

- Support both data discovery and data reuse.

- Keep data in motion, not at rest.

- Separate information delivery from data storage.

- Emphasize data transparency over data quality.

- Take an Agile approach to BI development.

It's this last point that has become the focus of a lot of controversy. Some BI practitioners have condemned the use of Agile methodologies in BI development. They claim that Agile approaches bypass the work of data transformation, data quality, metadata management, and data governance that are needed to make data reusable. These are valid concerns, and they will be addressed in this book.

However, I believe that the following characteristics of Agile approaches[1] are uniquely beneficial to BI projects:

- Agile methods have been shown to be effective for both maximizing value (through continuous delivery and prioritization of user stories) and minimizing risk (through face-to-face collaboration and time-boxed development cycles). Given the tremendous costs and significant risks involved in BI projects, an Agile approach is more than appropriate.

- Agile methods focus on collaboration between stakeholders. Again, this is a key aspect of any successful BI project, since the goal is to create data that people will use, and information that will be acted upon.

- Agile approaches give you "freedom to fail," which is essential in BI projects. As HP's Christopher Surdak has said, "To succeed at big data, you need to first do it wrong."[2] This is to say that BI is a journey, not a destination.

- An Agile system defines a "feedback loop" for each iteration of the project, requiring the end user to sign off on the project team's definition of "finished." This forces the project team to assess its work and continuously improve its processes.

This book will show you how to successfully navigate both the jungle of BI technology and the minefield of human nature. It will show you how to create a BI architecture and strategy that addresses the needs of all organizational stakeholders. It will show you how to maximize the value of your BI investments. It will show you how to manage the risk of disruptive technology. And it will show you how to use Agile methodologies to deliver on the promise of BI and analytics quickly, succinctly, and iteratively.

------

[1] For an explanation of the Agile methodology, please see Chapter 2 of my book *Building the Agile Database*, or take a look at the Agile Manifesto at http://www.agilemanifesto.org/principles.html.

[2] Surdak, Christopher. "Six Signs You're Going to Fail at big data." Information Management, August 12, 2015.

This book is about many things. But principally, it's about success. The goal of any enterprise initiative is to succeed and to produce benefits—benefits that all stakeholders can share in. I want you to be successful. I want your organization to be successful. This book will show you how.

This book is for anyone who is currently or will someday be working on a BI, analytics, or big data project, and for organizations that want to get the maximum value from both their data and their BI technology investment. This includes all stakeholders in the BI effort—not just the data people or the IT people, but also the business stakeholders who have responsibility for the definition and use of data. There are five sections to this book:

- In Section I, *What Kind of Garden Do You Want?*, we will examine the benefits and risks of Business Intelligence, making the central point that BI is a business (not IT) process designed to manage data assets in pursuit of enterprise goals. We will show how data, when properly managed and used, can be a key enabler of several types of core business processes. The purpose of this section is to help you define the particular benefit(s) you want your BI initiative to achieve, and set your BI target state goals.
    - o Chapter 1 examines the promise and perils of BI, and the importance of regarding BI as both a business process and an asset management process.
    - o Chapter 2 describes how data may be regarded and used as a business asset.
    - o Chapter 3 describes six fundamental types of business processes, and explains how BI can be an asset to each.
    - o Chapter 4 describes the general approach of iteratively implementing BI within the context of an overarching architectural vision.
    - o Chapter 5 describes the Agile methodology, and how it pertains to BI projects.
- In Section II, *Building the Bones*, we will talk about how to design and build out the "hardscape" (infrastructure) of your BI environment. This stage of

the process involves leveraging existing technology investments and iteratively moving toward your desired target state BI architecture.

- o Chapter 6 outlines an assessment of your existing technology investments and organizational culture.
- o Chapter 7 describes a pattern-based approach to iteratively moving from your "as-is" technology state to your BI target state.
- o Chapter 8 explores the process of "working toward" this desired BI target state through a gradual implementation of BI capabilities.

- In Section III, *From the Ground Up*, we explore the more detailed aspects of implementing your BI operational environment.
  - o Chapter 9 discusses the issues of data management, data quality, and metadata.
  - o Chapter 10 explores the use of data virtualization to produce multiple business information views from a single common set of data.
  - o Chapter 11 explains the difference between data and information, and the importance of basing your BI initiatives on data in motion, rather than data at rest. Several real-world examples of the business benefits of BI are given in this chapter.

- In Section IV, *Weeds, Pests, and Critters*, we talk about the many things that can go wrong on a BI project, and discuss ways of mitigating these risks.
  - o Chapter 12 catalogs common BI project risks and lists alternative mitigation approaches for each.
  - o Chapter 13 describes some of the human issues that can impact BI initiatives—companies ignore these human-centered BI risks at their peril!
  - o Chapter 14 explores why bad data drives out good data, and how good data can be made to drive out bad data.
  - o Chapter 15 addresses the issue of BI process bottlenecks and presents a set of Agile principles for identifying inefficient processes and either streamlining, automating, or eliminating them.

- In Section V, *The Sustainable Garden*, we talk about how to create a BI infrastructure that is easy and inexpensive to maintain.
    - Chapter 16 describes a set of operative principles for designing and building a sustainable BI environment.
    - Chapter 17 presents a list of "BI Critical Success Factors"—those things that should be done to ensure BI success.

- Finally, Section VI presents a case study illustrating the principles of this book, as applied to a fictional manufacturing company (the Blue Moon Guitar Company). This section also contains an afterword, the author's biography, a list of references and resources, description of key terms and acronyms, and a comprehensive index.

Key Points

- BI projects and programs face both technological and human obstacles. To be successful, technology decisions must be made, costs and risks must be managed, and human nature must be understood.

- The following core principles enable an organization to create a BI architecture and infrastructure that best suits the structure, culture, and stakeholder needs of their particular company:
    - Agile methodologies are uniquely suited to BI projects, enabling project stakeholders to identify value propositions and deliver on them quickly and iteratively, with minimal risk.
    - Agile methodologies enable project teams to fail quickly and (relatively) painlessly, as they determine the BI approach that is the best fit for their company.
    - Agile methods also inspire an attitude of continuous improvement and continuous delivery of value.
    - The Agile approach to BI is fundamentally about succeeding at whatever you do, in the best possible way.

Section I
What Kind of Garden Do You Want?

In my previous book, *Building the Agile Database*, I used landscape gardening as an analogy for how an Agile approach to IT projects should work. The landscaping metaphor is even more apt where BI is concerned, so I will be developing the analogy further in this book.

In this section, I'll address the fundamental question of what exactly business intelligence (BI) is, and what it means to an organization. Just as we wouldn't start the task of designing and creating a garden without some understanding of what we want from it, we shouldn't try to design and build BI infrastructure without knowing what we want our organization to achieve using BI.

In landscaping, everything starts from design; you don't just run out into the yard with a shovel and start digging. Neither do you start by running to the local nursery and buying a bunch of plants and plopping them into the ground. Either approach leads to a reckless garden; the result is, at worst, a lot of expensive dead plants, and at best, a garden that is unsatisfying and expensive to upkeep.

Similarly, many people take a reckless approach to BI: buying platforms, databases, and data visualization software, installing it all, and then trying to figure out how to use it. This usually results in vast expenditures of capital and few tangible business benefits.

Gardening expert Ann Lovejoy introduces the concept of "gardening by design" in the excellent book earlier acknowledged. Landscaping starts with a design that "takes into account our patterns of living, how we want to be in the garden, and what we want the garden to do for us."[3] In the world of BI, this means we should consider the information needs, challenges, and opportunities of a particular organization.

Landscape design must take into account the particular features and characteristics of the site, including soil type(s), drainage patterns, proportion of sun to shade, and so on. Every site and every landscape is different; a well-designed landscape will blend into its environment naturally. Furthermore, the scale of a well-designed garden always matches the scale of its environment; it is neither too big nor too small. There is no "one size fits all" solution, either in landscaping or BI. Every solution must be tailored to the realities of a specific location (or organization).

A good design makes a garden (and a BI environment) easily accessible and navigable, and satisfying and rewarding to utilize. It invites—it doesn't impose or impede. As Lovejoy puts it, good designs "have an elegant simplicity that makes them visually and emotionally pleasing even before a single plant is placed." Gardens are designed around space, not plants, in much the same way that musical composition centers around rests, not notes. Similarly, BI architectures are designed around the *usage* of data, not the data itself.

---

[3] Lovejoy, Ann. *The Handbook of Northwest Gardening* (Seattle: Sasquatch Books, 2003), Chapter 1.

Gardens contain access points and flow patterns, and consist of various "rooms" that satisfy different needs (entertainment, recreation, inspiration, introspection, etc.). Every room in a garden satisfies a different need; people are free to wander the garden at will until they find a room that meets their current need. Similarly, a BI environment needs to support multiple views and uses of data.[4]

Gardens are designed for intuitive ease of use. Nobody needs a user manual to tell them what to do in a garden. Likewise, a well-designed BI environment allows users to quickly and easily visualize and analyze their data in an intuitive way.

Gardens combine the right amount of inclusion (entertainment areas and open, decorative borders) with the right amount of privacy (screened areas and arbors for introspection and meditation). Similarly, in a well-designed BI architecture, data is made easily available to any authorized user, but protected from those who shouldn't see it.

Finally, a good design makes the landscape *sustainable*; that is, as the years go by, the benefits of the garden increase (as the landscape matures) but the amount of work and expense required to maintain it actually decreases. A well-designed landscape requires less fertilizing, less watering, and less overall maintenance with each passing year. Similarly, a well-designed BI environment should produce increased value with each passing year (as new data is added and new ways of reusing data and information are developed), while maintenance costs (after the initial learning curve is traversed) decrease.

By the end of this section, you should see the importance of starting your BI project with a design that takes into account the needs, goals, and processes of your organization. Just as we want to avoid creating gardens that are expensive and hard to maintain (and unsatisfying to experience), we want to avoid creating a BI infrastructure that consumes time, money, and resources without returning commensurate value to the enterprise.

---

[4] We'll examine this important concept in greater detail in Chapter 10.

Chapter 1
The Promise and Peril of BI

Those of us who have spent most of our careers toiling in the vineyards of data management should thank the purveyors of the new Big Data, BI, analytics, data visualization, and data virtualization products (after we finish cursing them for their daily telephone calls!). After decades of frustration, we are finally on the threshold of realizing the dream of data management: the ability to demonstrate to our companies the business value of high-quality, business-relevant, reusable data!

Even better, companies who previously hadn't spent so much as a cent on data or BI initiatives are now opening their wallets (and taking out second mortgages) to buy the latest and greatest BI and big data platforms and products. The company I currently work for, which hasn't spent a penny on a data or BI initiative in two decades, is now spending money like a sailor on shore leave!

Unfortunately, too many organizations are rushing into BI purchases and projects without giving five minutes' thought to what the end result should look like, and how it will be used. "Build it, and they will come" is a mantra that has been proven, time and time again on all manner of IT projects, to be dead wrong. Companies have spent millions of dollars building elaborate BI environments that ultimately go unused and produce no return on investment. Even worse, some companies have lost millions of dollars from bad business decisions based on the results of faulty analyses from these same BI systems![5]

This, in a nutshell, is the promise and peril of BI. On the one hand, BI promises significant revenue gains, increased market share, and reduced operating costs from rapid (even real-time) analysis of operational and social media data. On the other, we find abject (and expensive) failure when the final product either fails to deliver the promised results or when no one bothers to use it.

I can't think of a single IT-related initiative in which the chasm between possible success and possible failure is as deep and as wide as a BI initiative.[6] Indeed, it is this frightening chasm that has kept my current company from pursuing such an initiative in all these years. Now, however, the promised rewards are so great, and the technology so advanced, that even timid companies like mine are jumping on the BI bandwagon.

---

[5] Daragh O'Brien provides several examples of this in his TDAN article *Mitigate Information-Related Risks With Metadata* (TDAN.com, June 1, 2016). http://bit.ly/1WYQsEk. See also the Gartner report *The Data Lake Fallacy* (http://gtnr.it/1q8Nbia).

[6] It's hard to get solid statistics on BI failures, since it depends both on the approach taken to BI (e.g., data warehouse projects tend to fail more) and on how "failure" is defined (many BI projects deliver some value, but not the expected ROI). Nevertheless, published statistics on BI failure rates start at 50% (Gartner) and go up as high as 70%. A 2011 survey of 100 companies done by the UK's National Computer Centre found that 53% felt their company's BI project performance was "Average". 19% felt their BI projects met most or all business objectives, while 22% rated their company's BI project performance "Poor" or "Very Poor". The difficulty of integrating data from multiple source systems was listed as the primary cause of BI project failures.

THE QUESTION OF DATA MANAGEMENT

These new BI and big data products, however, are raising serious and troubling questions for those of us in data management. The promise of these new technologies, in essence, is that organizations can realize the benefits of BI and analytics without having to worry about data! No more mundane and troublesome tasks concerning data definition, modeling, quality, and governance. Just load all your data onto some storage platform, connect to it with a cool tool, and watch the moolah come rolling in!

These marketing ploys are actually not new. Many of us remember a time, about 15 years ago, when "data federation" was the buzzword of the day. Many companies were buying products that allowed them to perform analytics on their operational data in the source (application) databases, with no expensive and complicated data warehouses, data marts, or "Extract, Transform, Load" (ETL) processes. Unfortunately, those same companies quickly discovered that raw operational data from application-specific data stores can cause problems when fed directly into analytical processes. Many of the million-dollar BI failures alluded to earlier come from this period.

This is what many data management practitioners are really concerned about: not the use of Agile methodologies in BI per se, but the assumption that organizations can achieve the benefits of BI without having to worry about data. The new generation of BI products and tools are based on an assumption that business users are knowledgeable enough about data that they can do the work of data definition, cleansing, transformation, and governance, without having to involve IT. There may be some truth in this. However, we in data management must ask the following questions before making such assumptions:

- Do business users understand that they have taken on these roles? Are they equipped for them, and do they accept them?

- Is this work that business users (rather than IT crews) should be doing; that is, is this work an integral and value-added part of their job-related responsibilities? Several business users in our company spend significant amounts of their work time (and personal time) maintaining databases used for reporting and analytics. One engineer I spoke with spends 40% of her work time maintaining reporting data. Another admits to spending many evenings and weekends maintaining the database his group uses. Is this the best use of these people's time and abilities?

- What should be the proper role of IT in helping to ensure that business users have ready access to high-quality, reusable, business-relevant data? Where is the dividing line between delivering too little (of high quality) too late and delivering too much (of poor quality) too soon?

- Are we really empowering the business, or are we merely transferring the costs and risks associated with bad data (many of which are created by IT) from IT to the business?

- Do we have a proper understanding of the nature and degree of risk involved with this approach, and are there adequate controls in place to mitigate this risk? For example, what are the risks associated with individual business users cleansing or curating the same data in different ways and then sharing that data across the organization?

IMPORTANCE OF PROCESS

What really seems to be missing from this whole discussion of the "New BI" is any notion of *process*. Marketing for these new products is so focused on the capabilities and features of the platforms and tools, that we have given almost no thought to the business processes they support.

As previously mentioned, good design starts with an awareness and understanding of how the end product is meant to be used. (Remember the pivotal question: "how do we want to be in the garden, and what do we want the garden to do for us?") When designing a BI environment, the very first question we want to ask is, "How do we want people to use it, and what do we want them to get out of it?"

Think of it this way: if you were given the task of implementing an accounting system at your company, what would your first step be? Would you run out and buy some accounting software with a lot of cool features, install it, and expect people to start using it with ease? Of course not! You'd be better served by first talking to the stakeholders involved (i.e. the people who will actually use the system) and defining the type of accounting process that the system must support. Then you would be better prepared to select a product that best supports that process.

The difference between success and failure of a BI project, between realizing the benefits of BI and experiencing a devastating failure, lies in designing a BI environment that supports a clearly-defined and relevant business process.[7] There needs to be an understanding and acceptance of the roles that business people will assume in the support of these business processes (along with whatever training is required to help them fulfill these roles), and an understanding and acceptance of the role that IT teams will play.

Also remember that BI is, by its very nature, an asset management process which needs to be defined in the same way as other asset management processes (e.g. accounting, inventory, human resources). The goal of BI should be to maximize opportunities for use (and reuse) of assets and minimize the risks associated with mismanaging the assets (both the risks of doing the wrong thing with the assets and the risks of doing nothing at all).

Clearly, we need to thoughtfully and intelligently design a BI process that establishes the proper balance of roles, responsibilities, and risks between IT and the business. In the remainder of this section, I intend to define these various

---

[7] One objection to this contention is that BI can and should be used to identify new business processes that don't currently exist. My response would be that this falls under the heading of Innovation, which is most definitely a business process.

aspects of BI, and their respective roles and responsibilities. This is where the BI journey must start to ensure success.

Key Points

- Successful BI can yield significant benefits, including increased revenue and market share and decreased operating costs. However, BI projects also have significant costs and risks, and often fail to deliver the expected benefits.

- For success, there must first exist an understanding of the business processes that a BI environment will support, and an acceptance of this process (and its accompanying roles and responsibilities) by the business.

- A business must also clearly define the role that IT staff will play in introducing data into the BI environment, and the extent to which that data will be predefined, cleansed, transformed, and managed.

- The design of the BI environment should be informed by and support the defined business processes for reporting and analytics, as well as the roles that business users will assume in support of those business processes.

- BI is, by its very nature, an asset management process which should be defined in the same way as other asset management processes.

W e've already established that BI must support one or more defined business processes. Specifically, it should support asset management processes. The purpose of BI is to allow business users to manage and leverage their data assets in the same way as other business assets (capital, inventory, human resources, etc.). The question then becomes: what do these processes look like, and how should they work?

Actually, there are two other questions we must answer first:

- Is data, in fact, an asset according to the defined business meaning of the word?

- If so, what business benefits do we intend to enjoy from the effective management of this asset?

To answer these questions, we can turn to one of the seminal works in the field of data asset management: *The Information-Based Corporation* by David R. Vincent.[8] Readers of my earlier book will recognize the reference; Vincent has been one of the principal proponents of Stakeholder Economics, the principle upon which much of *Building the Agile Database* is based.

Vincent, in his book, makes the argument that data is a special type of asset, called a *circulating* asset (as opposed to fixed assets such as capital and inventory). Data meets the three essential characteristics of an asset, as defined by the Financial Accounting Standards Board:[9]

1. It can be managed for the benefit of an enterprise, either singularly or in combination with other assets.

2. A particular enterprise can obtain the benefit of the asset, and control access to it by other enterprises.

3. The transaction or event giving rise to the enterprise's right to control the asset has already occurred; that is, the investment has already been made and the asset is available for use.

However, as previously noted, data is a special kind of asset: circulating, rather than fixed. This means that data has the following additional characteristics:

1. It is *immutable*; that is, it is not consumed as it is used, and is therefore always available for additional reuse, up to the end of its useful life.

2. It is *copyable*; that is, it can exist in multiple places at the same time and can be used simultaneously by multiple people.

---

[8] Vincent, David R. The Information-Based Corporation: Stakeholder Economics and the Technology Investment. Homewood, Illinois: Dow-Jones-Irwin, 1990.

[9] Financial Accounting Standards Board, Statement of Financial Accounting Concepts No. 3: Elements of Financial Statements of Business Enterprises (Stamford, Conn., December 1980).

3. It is *indivisible*; that is, it must be used within a context that gives it meaning and business value.

4. It is *accumulative*; that is, data can be combined with other data and transformed into additional data assets at will.

These characteristics of circulating assets are the ones we need to keep in mind when designing BI systems. They represent the aspects of data that offer both the greatest potential value and the greatest potential risk. The right kind and type of data can be reused and combined with other data in an almost unlimited number of value-producing ways. On the other hand, the wrong kind of data (or data taken outside of its proper business context) carries any number of opportunities for a company to shoot itself in the foot. We will see numerous examples of both in this book.

However, data is also different from other kinds of assets. For one thing, there are fewer regulatory requirements (other than privacy requirements) associated with data. You can go to jail for giving someone a counterfeit bill or a bad check. Generally speaking, passing bad data doesn't land you behind bars.

There is a "fitness for purpose" aspect to data that doesn't exist for other assets. When you spend cash or liquidate stocks, you don't have to ask whether they are fit for the intended purpose. There's no need to ask, "Is this $20 bill good enough for this purchase?" With data assets, effort must be expended to ensure that their quality, currency, and relevance qualify them for the purpose for which they are being used. The question "is this data good enough?" must always be asked and answered.

One final point about asset management: generally speaking, what is being managed is not the asset itself, but the behavior of stakeholders regarding that asset. An accountant manages the way company employees track and document receipts and spending. An inventory manager controls when new inventory is ordered, and in what quantities. What data managers manage are the *processes* by which data assets are acquired, evaluated, enhanced, provisioned, used, and (eventually) disposed of, in ways that ensure the maximum amount of value is returned to the company. Asset management is never the management of things; it is always the management of people and processes.

Key Points

- Data is a special type of business asset, called a *circulating* asset (as opposed to a fixed asset, such as capital or inventory). Data meets the three essential characteristics of an asset, as defined by the Financial Accounting Standards Board.

- Data also has the four additional qualities of a circulating asset: it is *immutable*, *copyable*, *indivisible* and *accumulative*.

- The purpose of BI is to allow business users to manage and leverage their data assets in the same way as other business assets (capital, inventory, human resources, etc.) are managed.

- Fitness for purpose must always be considered when data assets are managed. A given set of data may be fit for one purpose, but unfit for another.

- Asset management is never the management of things; it is always the management of people and processes.

The biggest mistake that organizations make in the arena of Business Intelligence is to think of BI as a set of technologies or functions, rather than a set of business processes. Accounting, for example, is often thought of as a clerical function. In reality, accounting is a set of business processes that manages a collection of assets to fulfill enterprise objectives. Similarly, BI needs to be considered not just a technology that performs a business function, but as a set of processes that manages assets in support of business goals.[10]

In this chapter, we will outline a set of standard business processes and their objectives. Then, in subsequent chapters, we will map these business processes to a set of data management processes generally associated with BI:

---

[10] Some of the material in this chapter is taken from lectures in Business Data Management that I delivered at the University of Washington, Seattle, between 2001 and 2003.

- Data governance.
- Master data management.
- Metadata management.
- Records management.
- Data quality management.
- Data security management.

These processes are normally regarded as *impediments* to a successful BI project, to be avoided at all costs. As one business manager once said to me, "We're not interested in data quality or data governance or any of that IT stuff. Just give us the friggin' data!"

Certainly, the trend these days is to avoid anything that looks even remotely like process, and just give business users the "friggin' data" and let them fend for themselves. My contention, though, is that nothing independent of a business process will further a business objective, or provide measureable business value. I intend to demonstrate that these data management processes, when defined and implemented in the right way (that is, not as standalone IT processes but as sub-processes within standard corporate business processes) will provide greater business value than can be realized without them.

Let's start by considering BI not as a standalone business or IT function (which is usually how people think of it), but as an enabler of several standard business processes.

BI AS ASSET MANAGEMENT

As mentioned above, one of the principal benefits of BI is that it provides us (at long last) with an effective way to manage data as an enterprise asset. But what specifically do we mean by this?

According to the Institute of Asset Management (IAM)[11], there are three fundamental objectives of asset management:

1. Specific and measurable outcome or achievement required of asset system(s) in order to implement the asset management policy and asset management strategy.

2. Detailed and measurable level of performance or condition required of the assets.

3. Specific and measurable outcome or achievement required of the asset management system.

In other words, asset management encompasses not only management of the asset itself, but also management of the underlying business process and business strategy, and of the "system" (the specific implementation of tools or technologies) that supports the business process. Moreover, it must be possible to set specific and measureable goals for management of the asset, and to track progress toward those goals. This is one major reason why many BI projects fail to deliver on investment: they are not associated with specific and measureable business goals!

So what is it that we can measure and manage about an asset? The IAM notes the following as measureable characteristics of an asset:

- The cost of acquisition (the original cost of the asset).
- The quality of the asset.
- The business value of the asset.
- The cost of maintaining the value of the asset over time.
- The annual devaluation of the asset.
- The cost of eventual disposal of the asset.

In other words, we should be able to measure and manage the cost of acquiring, maintaining, and disposing of a business asset, as well as the value we obtain from it over time. We need to know when the cost of acquiring and/or maintaining the

---

[11] British Standards Institute, Publicly Available Specification BSI PAS55, 2008. http://bit.ly/2aa84IX.

asset exceeds its value, and when the useful or valuable life of the asset has expired. We also need to ensure that the quality of the asset is sufficient for the business need(s) it is intended to meet, and to recognize when it is not.

BI enables us to set and track measureable objectives for the management of *all* business assets (not only data). By defining and capturing appropriate *metrics* (measurements of key properties or characteristics of an asset), and tracking them against key performance indicators (*KPIs*) defined by the business, we can evaluate whether the business goals we have set for the asset are being met.

Many businesses use BI tools to create *dashboards*, which display the current set of metrics against KPIs in a visually accessible way, so that executives can tell at a glance which things are going well and which things are trending poorly. The effectiveness of a dashboard depends on a number of factors:

- The dashboard must measure the right things.
- The dashboard must measure to the right goals.
- The metrics must be trustworthy.
- The metrics must be actionable.
- The metrics must be actionable in a way that strengthens (not weakens) stakeholder relationships.

The annals of BI are filled with examples of BI initiatives that failed because the wrong metrics or KPIs were chosen, or because business executives couldn't accept what they were being told, or because the metrics drove the wrong behavior. As we will see throughout this book, almost any BI project can be a catastrophic failure if you don't keep business goals (and stakeholder needs) firmly in mind.

BI AS RISK MANAGEMENT

The principal objective of any enterprise is to maximize its opportunities while minimizing its risks. An enterprise always wants to find an appropriate and manageable balance between opportunity and risk. Since there is no opportunity without risk, it is important to understand both the critical success factors (i.e. those things that absolutely *must* happen for the project to succeed) and the significant risks (i.e. those things that absolutely *must not* happen, lest the project fail) from the outset. Think of a project or business initiative in terms of piloting a ship to a distant port: you must avoid rocks, shoals, and low water, keep sight of buoys and landmarks that help you track your position, sail with the winds as much as possible, and make sure you have sufficient fuel and provisions for the trip!

BI, then, provides us with the information we need to determine our position relative to the obstacles and landmarks, to chart the best course based on the prevailing wind, and to know at once if our fuel level is dangerously low.

Here's an example: some years ago, my wife and I were living in a geodesic dome house on Vashon Island. We decided to replace the front entrance of the house with a staircase rising from a small triangular deck off the driveway, up to a gallery running along the front of the house:

I'd built decks before, but never one quite like this, so I started by identifying the most significant potential process risk: that the house-facing side of the triangular deck would not be parallel to the house. This would mean that the staircase would be skewed and the treads would have to be cut wider on one end than on the other.

By measuring the distance between the house and each end of the house-facing side of the deck at regular intervals as I was building, I was able to ensure that the finished deck would be parallel to the house. This minimized the risk of what would have been, potentially, the most costly bit of "rework"– having to either move or rebuild the deck! Many other glitches occurred during the project, but by forestalling the major risk I was able to keep the other problems manageable and relatively inexpensive.

In short, risk management means always knowing how far you are from the things you are trying to avoid!

BI AS OPPORTUNITY MANAGEMENT

If risk management is like knowing how to sail safely from one port to another, opportunity management is knowing which port you want to sail to. All opportunities have potential benefits and actual costs (including the "opportunity cost" of not being able to do other things). It is important to be able to identify the potential opportunities that exist, evaluate the benefits of each opportunity relative to its cost, and decide which investment opportunities are mutually exclusive. This knowledge enables enterprises to invest their resources wisely, in opportunities that have the greatest potential for furthering their goals.

Examples of opportunity management include identifying new markets for existing products, new sales opportunities in existing markets, cross–selling and up–selling opportunities (to maximize the revenue potential of current customers), and monetization of assets and services (that is, identifying assets and services that can be sold to other parties at a profit).

BI can help organizations identify opportunities for using data and information to create what have been referred to as "virtual value chains"[12]: information-based

---

[12] See Michael E. Porter and Victor E. Millar, "How Information Gives You Competitive Advantage." Harvard Business Review, July–August 1985, pp. 149–160. Also see Jeffrey F. Rayport and John J. Sviokla, "Exploiting the Virtual Value Chain." Harvard Business Review, November–December 1995, pp. 75–85.

methods of linking stakeholders together in mutually value-enhancing ways. A classic example is American Hospital Supply (AHS), which created an online portal that enables its customers (doctors' offices and hospitals) to order products directly from its suppliers. AHS gets a percentage of each transaction and saves inventory and shipping costs, its suppliers get increased sales, and its customers get lower prices and faster service. AHS also benefits from a greatly improved relationship with both its suppliers and its customers.

Many other companies are using the power of BI and analytics to identify and take advantage of new business opportunities. For example, Express Scripts (an online pharmacy) enables subscribers to its online portal to manage their prescriptions and get useful information about medications they are taking. Express Scripts also uses analytics to proactively identify people who may not be taking prescribed medicine regularly, and works with them to resolve any problems they may be having (such as paying for the medications). This helps avert one of the fastest-growing costs in healthcare today: the cost of treating illnesses that arise from not taking prescribed medicine.

It is also true, as Stan Davis[13] has pointed out, that the economic value of information and knowledge is growing significantly faster than the value of traditional goods and services. As Davis puts it:

> *The more information you put into a product, or the more you are able to use a product to pull out information, the more you evolve beyond the original purpose into new ones. These new ones, which are based on information, may present even far greater opportunities than the original.*

Indeed, the packaging and marketing of information has become one of the principal wealth-generating activities of the modern economy. American Airlines, for example, makes more money from its SABRE reservations system (which it has sold to other airlines at a profit) than it makes from flying airplanes. Also, as

---

[13] Stan Davis and Bill Davidson. 2020 Vision: Transforming Your Business Today to Succeed in Tomorrow's Economy (New York: Fireside Books, 1991), pp. 17–18.

Thomas Davenport[14] notes, the distinction between physical and virtual value is rapidly disappearing—companies now sell their expertise to customers just as much as they sell goods and services. They sell "solutions" and "innovations," not just widgets.

To put it another way, BI enables businesses to not just sell more, but to serve more. It is in the identification of new opportunities to serve stakeholders that new opportunities for value and wealth are created.

BI AS PROCESS MANAGEMENT

The most essential characteristic of any organization in the new information economy is *Agility*: its ability to continually streamline, modify, or recreate its business processes on the fly, in response to changing business conditions and stakeholder needs.

Data is at the heart of most process improvement efforts, as exemplified by Six Sigma, a data-driven process improvement program used at many Fortune 500 companies. Data about a process (e.g. miles driven, resources used, time expended) is gathered and analyzed to find ways of optimizing that process.

UPS (United Parcel Service), for example, analyzes telemetric data from its trucks to streamline and optimize its delivery routes. To date, UPS has eliminated 364 million driver miles, saved 39 million gallons of fuel and eliminated 13,000 metric tons of emissions since 2001. UPS also uses telemetric data to identify drivers who need additional training (by detecting, for example, the number of times a driver backs up or makes a U-turn).[15]

---

[14] Thomas H. Davenport and Laurence Prusak. *Working Knowledge: How Organizations Manage What They Know* (Boston: Harvard Business School Press, 1998), pp. 13–14.

[15] http://bit.ly/2c5gS3u.

Companies, in order to be successful, must develop an appetite for experimentation, along with a "fail quickly" mindset. Processes need to be managed in a way that ensures that the inevitable failures will be as quick, painless, and inexpensive as possible. A combination of Agile methods and accurate up-to-the-minute data is the best way to ensure effective business processes.

BI AS STAKEHOLDER MANAGEMENT

In order to achieve its aims, an enterprise depends on the assistance, support, and cooperation of others. Customers, of course, are of primary importance, since their satisfaction justifies the existence of the enterprise. But other people are involved as well: employees, suppliers, investors, regulators, distributors, resellers, and more. All of these people must be kept informed of the needs and goals of the enterprise to ensure their support and cooperation.

Customers must be convinced to buy a product or service; suppliers must be convinced to supply high-quality goods and services at reasonable prices; investors and regulators must be convinced of the essential financial stability and integrity of the enterprise; distributors and resellers must be convinced to provide high-quality sales and support. Information helps us to nurture the relationships that ultimately determine the success of our efforts.

Business is all about conversation. Every business transaction is a dialogue between two or more business stakeholders, each of whom wants something from the other. Each conversation is driven by data, and the success of each transaction is determined by the ability of the data to move the stakeholders to an optimal and mutually satisfying outcome. BI should be about managing these conversations, not just managing the technology!

We have seen some examples of how information generated from BI processes can be used to add value to stakeholder relationships (e.g. AHS, Express Scripts). This reinforces the point made by David R. Vincent in his book *The Information-Based*

Corporation[16]: that in the new global economy, business value is created by establishing and nurturing relationships with business stakeholders.

He makes the further point that the essence of effective relationships lies in empowerment; that is, in giving people the ability to do more things for themselves. For example, from the comfort and convenience of my office, I can do all my banking, manage my investments, schedule my travel arrangements, look up information on almost any subject, and buy virtually anything anywhere in the world. BI technologies, generally speaking, have one thing in common: they use information to empower people at the lowest level of an organization. This flattens organizational hierarchies and eliminates intermediaries, resulting in much faster delivery of goods and services.

One aspect of stakeholder management is *branding*: the ways in which an enterprise creates for itself a unique identity and a message that conveys the value it provides to its customers. It includes identifying the wants and needs of potential customers in each demographic group, and distinguishing its products and services from those of its competitors. This is an area in which BI is particularly useful, enabling companies to identify the ever-changing preferences of individual demographic groups, and to tailor its brand identification and message to each specific group. In our increasingly diverse and dynamic society, effective branding is essential to the survival of any organization.

BI AS KNOWLEDGE MANAGEMENT

Finally, BI provides us with an effective means of generating and sharing data and information in a way that, over time, adds significantly to an organization's storehouse of knowledge and expertise. This is an important aspect of BI, and one that's usually neglected by its practitioners. Too much of the BI activity in our organizations is limited to individuals or departments analyzing data and creating data products.

---

[16] Ibid.

What's missing from this limited scope is the sharing of these individual insights across the organization in a way that enriches organizational understanding, improves organizational agility, and enhances organizational capabilities. Insights gained through BI need to be shared as widely as possible, to ensure that individuals and departments aren't doing the same analysis of the same data, duplicating efforts, and possibly creating competing views of the truth. Information that is shared is more likely to be reused, thus enabling organizations to leverage what they know now to achieve greater knowledge and expertise later.

Key Points

- BI needs to be considered not just a technology that performs a business function, but as a set of processes that manages assets in support of business goals.

- BI needs to map business-based asset management processes with IT-based data management processes.

- Asset management encompasses not only management of the asset itself, but also management of the underlying business process and business strategy, and of the "system" (the specific implementation of tools or technologies) that supports the business process.

- Metrics and KPIs can be used to set and track measureable objectives for the management of all business assets (not only data). However, for metrics to be effective, they must be measuring the right things, measuring to the right goals, and driving the right behavior.

- Business processes that can be managed using BI include asset management, risk management, opportunity management, process management, stakeholder management, and knowledge management.

Chapter 4
Achieving the BI Vision

We have now identified a few critical characteristics of BI:

- It must support one or more defined business processes.
- It must combine business-based asset management processes with IT-based data management processes.
- It must support the right mix of value-added work from both IT teams and the business.
- It must provide measureable business value.
- It must produce actionable insight.

With these criteria in mind, we can begin to map out our vision of how we want to implement BI in our organization and reap its benefits.

As with landscaping, we need to have both a long-term vision and a set of short-term goals. You can't just say, "This year, I'm going to create a garden that makes the centerfold of *Sunset* magazine." That may be your long-term vision, but it's not immediately achievable. Your short-term goals will be more on the order of: "I'll set the herbaceous borders this year, and put the patio in next year." However, each of these smaller, short-term projects must be done within the context of the overall architecture and design of the garden (this is what Ann Lovejoy calls "Working Toward"), and each project must iteratively move the landscape closer to its ultimate vision.

With BI, your long-term vision (what we call the *target state architecture*) needs to accommodate several sets of short-term goals, including the creation of the BI infrastructure, the gathering (and probably cleansing) of data, the definition of business processes, the creation of business metrics, the demonstration of business value, and the enlisting of both business and management support. A reasonable set of BI goals for a three-month period might look something like this:

- Implement a data visualization/analysis tool in one department or division.
- Define a few metrics that the department/division wants to capture and track.
- Identify the data needed to create the requested metrics.
- Provision the necessary data (cleansing if necessary).
- Apply the visualization/analysis tool to the data to create the metrics.
- Assess the effect of the metrics on one or more business processes and determine their business value.
- Demonstrate the visualizations, metrics, and business benefits to business management, to enlist support for the next iteration of the process.

This is roughly the approach we are taking toward the implementation of BI at my company, and one that will be immediately familiar to anyone who has worked on an Agile project. The essence of an Agile approach is that it manages risk by ensuring that some defined piece of business value will be delivered within a manageable period of time, at a reasonable cost. Or, if not, at least the project will fail quickly, and with minimal fiscal pain.

The challenge is ensuring that the accretion of these "quick wins" moves your organization iteratively toward its longer-range vision: a BI infrastructure that makes trustworthy and reusable data quickly and easily available across the organization, supporting the improvement of all of its business processes, and enabling the growth and sharing of knowledge and expertise across the enterprise. This is why it's important to plan these short-term projects in the context of a clearly-defined overarching architecture and design. After each project is completed, it should be assessed to make sure it:

- Delivered the expected business benefits.
- Fit within the defined architecture.
- Moved the organization toward its BI vision.

This assessment will help the organization make changes in approach, eventually causing future projects to deliver benefits more effectively. It will also lead to a reassessment of the long-term BI vision: should our long-term vision change? Should our strategy change? Should our architecture change?

The architectural context of the BI vision will be the topic of the next section. We will examine a number of pattern-based approaches for implementing short-term BI projects while iteratively moving toward a longer-range BI vision.

Key Points

- An organization needs to have both a long-term vision for what it wants to achieve from a BI initiative, and a set of short-term goals that moves the organization iteratively toward that vision.

- All BI projects should be planned within the context of an overarching BI architecture and design, to ensure that each project contributes meaningfully to the ultimate objective.

- An Agile approach ensures that each BI project contributes measureable value to the business and fits correctly into the defining architecture.

- Each BI project should be assessed after completion to determine whether it delivered the promised business benefits, fit into the defined BI architecture, and moved the organization toward its BI vision.

- After each project, the BI vision and architecture can be reassessed to determine if any changes or adjustments are needed.

Before I move on to the topic of BI Architecture, I feel it necessary to address some of the current misconceptions around "Agile" BI. As previously mentioned, some data management professionals feel that Agile precepts are antithetical to the data management work necessary to make BI a success. Others feel that the Agile process does nothing more than add an additional layer of process on top of existing BI processes. Neither of these concerns is necessarily true, although both of them need to be understood and addressed.

Other concerns come from Agile practitioners themselves: Dave Thomas, one of the principal authors of the "Agile Manifesto,"[17] now advocates abandoning the concept of Agile (as a noun or an adjective) in favor of the concept of Agility (as a

---

[17] "Manifesto for Agile Software Development", http://www.agilemanifesto.org/.

verb).[18] Agility, properly understood, (Thomas says) involves nothing more intricate than taking the following simple steps:

- Find out where you are.
- Take a small step towards your goal.
- Adjust your understanding based on what you learned.
- Repeat.

In other words, Agile is not so much a defined methodology as much as it is a way of working (or of thinking about working). Note that while "Agility" is a commonly-accepted business concept, the use of the term "Agile" (as an adjective) is virtually non-existent outside of IT. You never, for example, hear people refer to themselves as "Agile bankers" or "Agile carpenters" or "Agile CPAs". You don't see people outside of IT going to conferences and seminars to learn SCRUM-based techniques for, say, home remodeling or gardening.

Why? Because everybody outside of IT knows how work is supposed to get done! This is why I use landscape gardening and home remodeling as metaphors for Agile processes. In these endeavors, you start with a goal (or design) in mind. You then use what you currently know to take the first steps toward that goal. Next, you evaluate both your process (to identify improvements) and your goal (to see whether it needs to change). Finally, you use that knowledge to take the next steps toward the revised goal, and start the cycle all over again. Eventually, you get to a point that may not exactly correspond with your original goal, but is where you realize you needed to end up. That's the finish line—for now.

Another objection to the Agile concept comes from practitioner Wayne Kernochan. His article[19] makes a number of excellent points about Agile BI, but the most important is that BI and analytics in themselves are not Agile; they merely reflect the degree to which the businesses that use them are (or are not) Agile.

---

[18] Thomas, Dave. "Agile is Dead (Long Live Agility). Blog posting, March 4, 2014, http://bit.ly/2amZ9Hx.

[19] Kernochan, Wayne. "What Agile Business Intelligence Really Means." Blog posting, April 7, 2011, http://bit.ly/2aa7ydI.

Organizations that are capable of rapid, effective, fact-based decision-making are likely to derive significant benefit from BI and analytics processes. Organizations hampered by excessive organizational hierarchies, process-bound management, and "gut-based" decision-making will not—no matter how much BI and analytics technology they have at their disposal.

Wayne makes the additional point that BI, in order to be considered truly "Agile," can't just focus on optimizing the value of existing data and business processes. It must possess the ability to seek out new sources of useful data, get information to key decision-makers quickly, and identify needed changes in those business processes (including the need to abandon them).

The importance of an Agile approach to BI is this: Agile processes essentially manage *work*, to ensure that the right work (and *only* the right work) is done at the right time by the right people in the right way. Work is managed in order to reduce *risk*—for example, the risk (and cost) of doing work that isn't needed, or not needed now, or that will need to be abandoned or done over later.

Risk must be managed in order to maximize *opportunity*—defined as the ability of organizations to take advantage of *change* (changes in business climate, changes in market conditions, changes in customer needs, and changes in technology). As previously noted, an Agile approach to BI is necessary because BI represents the perfect intersection of risk (what we currently don't know and can't do) and opportunity (what we must know and be able to do in order to be successful).

Agile is essentially a journey of discovery, wherein an organization gradually and iteratively tests the limits of its knowledge and understanding and grows them into new arenas of endeavor. This is a journey fraught with both opportunity and risk, and must be taken a step at a time. At each step in the process, one of two things must happen: either some piece of BI value is successfully delivered to one or more business customers, or else a small, quick, inexpensive, manageable failure (let's call it a "learning experience") occurs. At no point in the journey should you "fall off Mount Everest". Manage the risk so that it doesn't swallow up the opportunity. This is the essence of Agile.

Key Points

- Agile involves envisioning a goal, and taking small incremental steps to reach it. At each step, you evaluate both the process (to identify improvements) and the goal (to see whether it needs to change). Then you use that knowledge to take the next few steps toward the (revised) goal, and so on.

- Agile manages *work*, so as to maximize *opportunity* and minimize *risk*.

- Agile is essentially a journey of discovery, wherein an organization gradually and iteratively tests the limits of its knowledge and understanding and grows them into new arenas of endeavor.

- At each iteration of an Agile process, one of two things must happen: either some piece of value is successfully delivered to one or more business customers, or else a small, quick, inexpensive, manageable failure occurs.

- An Agile approach to BI is necessary because BI represents the perfect intersection of risk (what we currently don't know and can't do) and opportunity (what we must know and be able to do in order to be successful).

Section II
Building the Bones

O nce we know what we want to accomplish with our garden (i.e. "how we want to be in the garden, and what we want the garden to do for us"), the next step is the design of the garden itself. In landscape design, we start with what's called the "hardscape": the underlying structure of paths, walkways, beds, patios, seating areas, ponds, and arbors that form the structure of the landscape. Each one of these features should support the functionality of each part of the garden (for example, a serene view or water feature for contemplation, or a deck or patio for entertaining). In landscaping terms, this is called "building the bones" of the garden.

One of the most fundamental challenges of BI, in my opinion, is the difficulty of creating this "hardscape." Unless you're fortunate enough to work for a company that adheres to good data management principles (master data management, business metadata, enterprise data models, data governance, etc.), you'll likely find yourself in the unenviable position of being asked to build a car while people are driving it!

This is the position I currently find myself in. In our company, which doesn't "do" data management, everybody wants to jump into the pool of BI exploration and analytics. Unfortunately, we haven't yet built the pool. Or dug the hole for the pool. Or even hired anyone to dig the hole or build the pool. Nevertheless, everyone in our company wants to go swimming—*now!*

This disconnect between what we want (or need) and what we currently have is one of the most important drivers for an Agile approach to BI development. Your business users are not going to wait for years while you conduct stakeholder interviews, create an enterprise data model, design and build an enterprise data warehouse, and institute an organization-wide data governance framework. Like it or not, you're going to have to find some way of getting your business users some "quick wins" with the data and infrastructure you currently have, while mapping out a strategy (and drumming up support) for a longer-term BI vision.

In this section, we'll take a look at some Agile approaches to constructing a "play as you go" BI architecture, including the use of BI patterns.

O ne of the first steps in creating a landscape is doing an assessment of the property. When I design a landscape, I walk over the entire property a number of times, carrying a sketch pad, colored pencils, and a camera. I note the topography of the property, its hills and slopes. I note the movement of the sun across the property. I identify trees and shrubs that need to be kept, trees and shrubs that need to be moved, and trees and shrubs that need to be removed. I note the locations of power lines, water lines, septic tanks, and more. I note existing features such as patios, decks, and storage sheds. Most importantly, I note points of access, points of movement, and points of stability (e.g. places where people might want to sit, congregate, or meditate).

Similarly, one of the first steps in creating a BI infrastructure is an assessment of your current BI and data environment. What data do you have that might be valuable for BI and analytics purposes? Where is it? Is the data easy or difficult to access? What DBMSs (database management systems) does your organization currently support? What applications are used to create the data? Who in the organization is responsible for overseeing the creation of that data? What, if any, BI activity is currently occurring in your organization and where and how is it being done? What is the quality of the data in your organization? What BI structures (data warehouses, master data stores, data marts, OLAP cubes, etc.) currently exist that might be leveraged? What data models (if any) exist in your organization, and how current and comprehensive are they? What external data does your company have access to that might have value when combined with internal data?

The assessment should also include a list of political, organizational, and budgetary constraints. How much money will management make available to support a BI initiative? How much support from executive management can be counted on? What personnel resources will be made available? In what timeframe are results expected? Who will be held responsible (on both the IT side and the business side) for results?

Another question to ask is whether your company's management is locked into solutions from a particular vendor or vendors. If so, this will constrain the BI architecture you are allowed to create. Are there political or organizational constraints to consider (for example, a central IT organization that must approve all data or BI infrastructure, or managers who regard BI as "their turf")?

One fact that must be accepted is that there is no "Data Fairy," no magical elves that will instantly create a BI infrastructure for you. A BI initiative, like any other type of work, requires people, money, and competent management. Companies that are willing to staff and fund, for example, a BI Competency Center (BICC) are much more likely to achieve BI success more quickly than a company that believes it can manage this work within existing staffing and funding. Everybody wants their garden to look like the ones in *Sunset* magazine, but those gardens are usually created by professional contractors and landscapers who are paid many thousands of dollars. Expectations need to be kept realistic.

You will also want to check with your business users to get a sense of how they are currently using, and how they would like to use, data to perform business analysis and business decision-making. What sorts of data visualizations do they need to do? What sorts of analysis? How will the results of these analyses be communicated to others, both inside and outside the company? What tools are they comfortable using? What sort of user training might be needed? What documentation (including metadata) is needed to support their work?

You will want to think about the business processes that your BI initiatives will support, or transform, or replace. Which current business processes could be made more effective by applying a BI effort? What business processes could be created from newly-available data and information, and what sort of business value could these processes return? What new business capabilities would you like to create? What new data capabilities or services could you create and monetize?

You will also want to think about people. Who are the data, BI, and business subject matter experts (SMEs) at your company? Whose expertise and assistance will you need to help make your BI initiatives successful? How available are these people? Are contract or vendor resources available to help you?

When we started our company's BI initiative, one of the first things we did was a number of one-month proof of concepts (POCs), using different tools and approaches. We involved business users (as well as vendors) in each POC. The idea was to get a sense of how many resources (such as time, money, and energy) would be needed to deliver results to the business, and how easy or difficult it would be for business users to create value from what was delivered.

Using this approach, we were able to identify a particular data visualization and analysis tool that our business users were not only comfortable with but excited about using, and identify approaches to BI that were workable within our resource and budget constraints. Importantly, we were also able to identify approaches that wouldn't work for us. For example, we rejected an OLAP-based approach because of the time and effort needed to design and create dimensional data structures, write the ETL to populate them, and iteratively modify the cube structures based on constantly changing user requirements.

At the same time, we also rejected a "dump all the data onto a server and run" approach because, long term, we wanted to create a store of integrated, organization-wide data that could support applications (especially Cloud-based applications) and service-oriented architecture (SOA) web services as well as BI and analytics. We recognized that, although we might have to settle for sub-optimal data in the short term, the greatest value for the company would ultimately be realized by creating data that was integrated, trustworthy, and reusable across our business units.

However, we also rejected the traditional data warehouse approach, for a number of reasons. First, the term "data warehouse" conjures up a vision of a repository of static (and therefore out-of-date) data waiting for somebody to come along and figure out how to apply it to a business problem (one that has already occurred, and thus resides in the past). We needed the capability to capture and analyze data in real time, and in motion.[20] As previously mentioned, we wanted our integrated data repository to support applications and web services as well as BI and reporting. Also, data warehousing is associated with a number of processes (in particular, ETL and the creation of semantic metadata) that are arduous, time-consuming, resource-intensive, and expensive.[21]

What we decided we needed was a target state architecture that would enable us to quickly and easily capture, analyze, integrate, reuse, and act on any data, in any form, wherever it might exist.

Once we determined what we needed, it was time to sit down and figure out how we could get from here to there.

---

[20] This is sometimes known as Complex Event Processing, or CEP.

[21] This topic will be explored in more detail in Chapter 15.

BI Assessment Checklist

- Data:
    - What data will be most valuable to your organization?
    - Where is the most authoritative source of this data?
    - How trustworthy and reliable is this data?
    - What needs to be done to put this data into a trustworthy state?
    - Who is responsible for the creation and oversight of this data?
    - What data models exist, and how good are they?
    - What data external to your organization would be of value?
- Technology:
    - On what DBMSs and platforms does your current data reside?
    - How accessible is this data?
    - Are there any licensing issues around the access of this data?
    - Are any current BI data structures in use?
- Vendors:
    - With which data/database/BI vendors do you already have relationships?
    - With which vendors would you feel most/least comfortable partnering?
    - Which vendors would be willing to support a POC at your company?
    - Are there vendors your company refuses to partner with?
    - Are there vendors your company requires you to use?
- Business:
    - How do your business users want to access and work with data?
    - What are their BI/analytics goals and visions?
    - What BI tools are your business users most comfortable using?
    - What sorts of analyses, forecasting, reporting, and visualizations do your business users want/need to do?
    - What metadata (information about the data) will they need in order to use data effectively, and with minimal risk and uncertainty?

- Management:
    - What budget and resources are likely to be made available to support a BI initiative?
    - Is management receptive to the idea of establishing a BI Competency Center (BICC)?
    - What level of management support can be expected for a BI initiative?
    - In what timeframe are results from a BI initiative expected?
    - What organizational metrics and KPIs exist, and must be supported by a BI solution?
    - What organizational metrics and KPIs should be created?
- Process:
    - What current processes could be improved or replaced by a BI initiative?
    - What new business processes or capabilities could be created?
    - What new data or services could be created and monetized?
- People:
    - Who are the data, BI, and business subject matter experts (SMEs) in your organization?
    - What is the availability of these people?
    - Are contract or vendor resources available?
- Company Culture:
    - To what extent do new technology initiatives require approval or support from central IT?
    - To what extent are business divisions able to undertake their own IT and BI projects?
    - What sort of oversight and reporting will be required for BI initiatives?
    - Who (in IT and the business) will be held accountable for results?
    - Are there political or organizational (e.g. "turf") constraints to consider?
    - What sort of data governance organization/process exists, and how is it implemented?

Key Points

- A realistic assessment of your current data and BI environment is a crucial first step in developing your BI architecture.

- This assessment should include political, organizational, and budgetary constraints that may limit possible design options, as well as current and future vendor relationships.

- The assessment should also include interviews with business stakeholders to determine how they are currently using, and how they would like to use, data to perform business analysis and business decision-making.

- Consideration should be given to the business process that will be created, transformed, improved, or eliminated as the result of BI initiatives, as well as to the people available and needed to support these initiatives.

- An Agile approach to BI development will include several short Proof of Concept (POC) projects designed to identify the best and most cost-effective ways of provisioning data and performing data visualizations and analytics.

- Adequate staffing and funding for the work of developing the BI architecture is essential to success.

An Agile approach to anything (including landscape gardening) is based on recognizing patterns. We always try, as much as possible, to avoid reinventing the same wheel over and over again—this wastes time and effort that should be applied to more value-producing work!

Data modelers have long used patterns as jumping-off points when modeling familiar data subject areas.[22] They are also commonly used in application development. However, we have not yet seen patterns used much in BI architecture.

As noted in previous chapters, we have two different problems that need to be solved simultaneously: we need to begin delivering immediate business value

---

[22] For an excellent exposition of the use of data model patterns in Agile development, please see John Giles' book, *The Nimble Elephant* (2012, Technics Publications LLC, Westfield NJ USA).

from our BI initiative, using the data and infrastructure we already have, while incrementally building out our long-range BI target state. The judicious use of patterns enables us to achieve both goals.

This chapter will present a series of BI patterns, which should be regarded as a progression. That is, starting with the first pattern leads (in time) to the next, then to the next, then to the next. Not all organizations will use all of these patterns, nor will they progress through the patterns in the same order. Any given pattern will be designed and implemented differently from one company to the next, and will use different technologies.

The idea here is not to prescribe an ideal approach to BI, but rather to suggest pathways that can enable any given organization to get from where they currently are to where they would like to be. And, of course, each organization will have a different idea of what its target-state BI goal should look like. The purpose of the patterns is to help organizations along the path toward that goal as quickly as possible.

PATTERN 1: QUICK WINS

In this pattern, we start with a data visualization product (e.g. Tableau or Microsoft Power BI). Spreadsheet or file-based data is used as-is, or with minimal cleansing and transformation, from central IT databases and local servers. Data is either connected directly by the visualization tool, or copied onto the data visualization server to create data sources that business users can use for reporting and analysis. This pattern is represented graphically on the facing page.

With this approach, it is usually necessary to create read-only copies of production data sources, to ensure that production applications aren't adversely impacted by BI, reporting, and analytics queries. A "view layer" on top of the database schemas helps to insulate the BI processes from changes in the underlying schema, gives users a more business-friendly representation of the data, helps improve query performance, and can facilitate some initial integration, cleansing, and reformatting of the data.

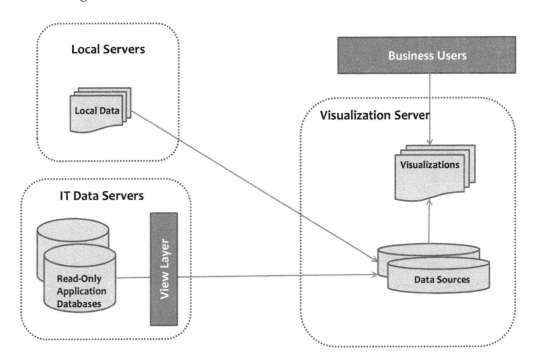

An alternative approach is to make use of a data virtualization/data federation platform (e.g. Composite/Cisco or Denodo) to pre-integrate the multiple data sources and present them as a unified set of abstracted data views to the visualization server, as shown on the next page.

The advantage to this alternative approach is that it creates a more integrated, robust, and powerful data source for the visualization server, and may eliminate the need to create read-only copies of production data sources. Also, the view layer that supports the integration, cleansing and reformatting of the data resides (and is supported) in one place, rather than in multiple application databases.

As with any pattern, there are advantages and shortcomings to its application in any given situation. In each case, we must ask the following questions:

- What are the advantages of using this pattern in this situation?
- What are the drawbacks or risks?

- When can and can't this pattern be used?
- How can the risks of using this pattern in this situation be mitigated?
- What caveats do we need to keep in mind when applying this pattern?

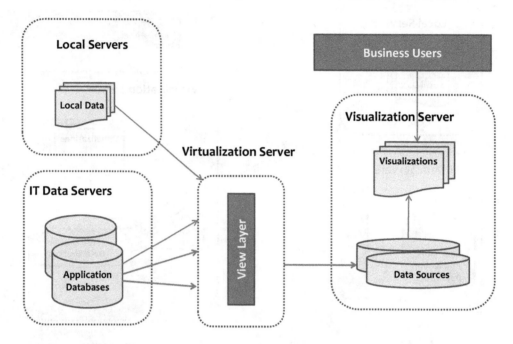

The key advantage of the pattern above is that it delivers some measure of initial business value quickly, at minimal expense, and with a minimum of IT involvement. It enables business users to begin familiarizing themselves with their BI tool and with their data, and allows the business to define its BI requirements and needs without spending a lot of time and money. Moreover, this approach helps generate enthusiasm and support on the business side for further BI investments.

The drawbacks to this pattern are well-understood: it requires the business to use data that is defined in application (IT) terms, not business terms. A given piece of data may not mean the same thing to an application as it does to the business. Data quality will likely be problematic. Accessing data in application databases may impact the performance of transactional systems. Finally, this pattern doesn't address the problems or opportunities of creating a cross-organizational integrated business view of a company's data.

We can mitigate some of these drawbacks by off-loading application data onto a replication server (as with Microsoft SQL Server transactional replication), onto the server supporting the data visualization tool, or onto a data virtualization server.

We can also interpose a view layer (called an "information view") between the data and the business users. As we shall see, the information view is a very important component of all these patterns. It enables us to create a business-friendly and usable representation of the source data; allows us to do at least a minimal amount of data cleansing, integration, and reformatting; and enables us to more easily transition our BI architecture from one pattern to the next.

In summary, use this pattern when:
- Initial BI value needs to be delivered quickly.
- Business information requirements need to be defined before major investments of time and money are made.
- Users want to become familiar with the BI tools.
- Initial data exploration and discovery need to be done.

Pros:
- Minimal IT resources required; no data structures (e.g. data warehouses or data marts) needed.
- Allows the business to define how they want to analyze before large amounts of time and money are spent.
- Facilitates data exploration, data discovery, and data profiling, giving the business (and IT) a better understanding of how the value and reliability of the data can be improved.

Cons:
- Data is defined in application/IT (not business) terms.
- Data quality may be problematic.
- Read-only copies of production data sources may need to be created.

Caveats:

1. Beware of directly accessing data in production transactional databases, as this may adversely impact the performance of these applications. If you can, replicate the data to a read-only copy; otherwise, you might be able to ameliorate the problem using database views. Views can restrict the amount of data that can be returned from a single query, they can ensure that only authorized users can access the data, and they can use hints (e.g. a NOLOCK hint) to reduce the amount of database locking done by a query.

2. Be aware that raw application data may not be suitable for all business information purposes. At least some minimal cleansing and transformation of the source data may be required. For database data, you might be able to use views, or a combination of views and table-valued functions, to accomplish this. Some of the risk of using raw application data can be offset through the use of metadata (more on metadata in a moment).

3. This pattern is more likely to be successful when used against data from a single source, as opposed to data from multiple sources that must be integrated. If data from multiple sources must be integrated, be sure that the data sets pertain to similar or related business entities defined in similar terms, and that the data is integrated based on commonly-defined key attributes. In other words, make sure you're joining apples to apples, not apples to oranges![23]

A major goal of this pattern is to eliminate dependence on IT as much as possible while BI requirements are developed and solidified, data sources are identified, and data is examined for suitability of purpose. After the requirements have been developed and the visualizations solidified, the supporting data can be cleansed

---

[23] In one example of what can go wrong, a business analyst tried to blend two sets of customer data – one set was keyed on Customer ID, which turned out to be a surrogate key, and the other was keyed on Customer Number, which turned out to be a billing account number.

and transformed as necessary, and moved to an enterprise data repository for reuse across the organization.

Note: This pattern is probably what most people think of as "Self-Service BI." However, it should be noted that *all* of the patterns in this book are designed to support the end goal of self-service BI; they just do so in different ways.

To date, my company has realized more than $8 million in business benefits (mostly from process improvements) from the use of this pattern.

PATTERN 2: FORKLIFT

In this pattern, data from central and division IT servers is "forklifted" (i.e. moved in its native form, with a minimum of cleansing and transformation) to some sort of high-performing "data appliance." Generally speaking, the pattern looks like this:

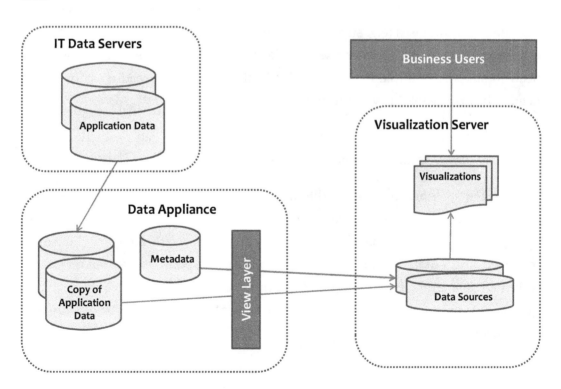

There are at least three different approaches to this pattern. The approach your team chooses will be determined mostly by deciding where, in your long-term BI target state architecture, the bulk of your reusable enterprise-wide data will reside. In other words, this pattern is the first step toward building out your eventual enterprise data repository and associated metadata.

This is where you must answer the question: "What kind of garden do you want?" What do you want your enterprise-wide BI architecture to look like, and what do you want it to do? Where and how does an enterprise-wide data repository (of some sort) fit into this architecture? How trustworthy is your enterprise data in its native state? To what degree are you going to need to manage (i.e. cleanse, transform, and curate) your data to make it reusable and trustworthy across your organization? Or, if you're not going to manage your data, then how will you ameliorate the risk of using non-curated data for enterprise-level decision-making?

Another important question: how will your data be consumed, and by whom? Will your data be used only for BI, analytics, and reporting purposes, or will it be intended for other uses (e.g. support for applications and/or web services) as well? If only for BI, will your BI users use a single standard tool, or does your BI solution need to support multiple end-user tools? Will your data be read-only, or will it need to be updateable? If so, how and by what means?

As I said earlier, there are at least three different ways you can proceed: let's call them the *Schema, Schema Lite,* and *No Schema* approaches.

In the *Schema* approach, the forklifted data is put into tables in some sort of relational DBMS. You would take this approach if you intended to create an enterprise ODS (operational data store) or EDW (enterprise data warehouse) of managed and curated data. The tables would correspond to the layout of the forklifted data, and would likely not be normalized; the idea here would be just to get the data onto the eventual target platform in a way that could be quickly and easily consumed.

A view or views would be created on top of these tables in order to present the data for consumption by the data visualization tool. Later, when the data was cleansed, reformatted, and moved to the enterprise data repository, these views would be repointed to the new data store, thus minimizing the impact of the data re-hosting on the BI end users. The existing "forklift" tables would be repurposed as *Staging* (or *Landing Pad*) tables used as part of the ELT (Extract, Load and Transform) process of moving data from source systems into the ODS or EDW.

In the *Schema Lite* approach, the forklifted data is moved to a non-relational data appliance such as Qlik or SAP's HANA. These platforms use complex columnar-based indexing algorithms and in-memory data storage to link data sources together and feed the data quickly to the end user. There is a minimal schema required to get the data loaded onto the appliance, but it is not normalized.

The data design, as such, is achieved in the view layer that is interposed between the end user and the data. The consumption of the data (for reporting, BI, and analysis) is completed using visualization tools specific to the appliance (e.g. Qlik's QlikView and SAP's Lumira). Use this approach if you are not going to create an enterprise ODS or EDW, if data will be consumed using only the appliance's visualization tool, and if the data is going to be only minimally managed or curated. Note that SAP's HANA appliance can also be used to support SAP's ERP applications, as well as its business warehouse (SAP/BW).

In the *No Schema* approach, data is loaded in native form onto a Hadoop cluster (or, alternatively, a NoSQL data store of some sort). The idea is to simply persist the data somehow, in a way that doesn't require the data to be organized into a schema. This does, however, present the problem of accessing the data and putting it into a form that can be quickly and easily searched, integrated with other data sources, and consumed by end users.

Usually, some sort of data virtualization engine is required for this work. This can be one of the commercial DV products (such as Composite/Cisco or Denodo), a product created specifically for the target data environment (such as Hive for Hadoop, which gives users a relational view of data stored in Hadoop's HFS file system, and allows them to query the data using SQL-like syntax), or an open source solution such as Unity[24], which supports SQL-like integration and querying of both SQL and NoSQL data.

The goal of this pattern is to quickly get data from multiple sources onto the data platform that's at the center of your BI architecture and strategy, and to put that data to use as quickly as possible. This may be the point at which your BI strategy stops (if you don't intend to move on to any of the other patterns, and don't intend to do any data management). Ideally, though, this pattern is a way-stop, an intermediate step toward the eventual end goal of a multi-functional enterprise data repository and BI strategy.

Use this pattern when:
- You want to transition your organization's data onto your eventual target state data platform.
- You want to get some "quick wins" with the new platform to justify its cost and generate end-user acceptance and support.
- You want to use data that is currently inaccessible (e.g. on a mainframe or local server), or for which no read-only copy is available.
- Accessing data remotely (as in the "Quick Wins" pattern) results in unacceptably poor BI performance.
- A quick proof of concept (POC) needs to be created to demonstrate the business value of BI.

Pros:
- Data can be provisioned fairly quickly in response to urgent business needs.
- Data is moved away from production transactional systems and databases.
- Putting the data on a data/database appliance results in greatly increased performance.

---

[24] http://bit.ly/2aqLOfz.

- Data aggregations and integrations can be represented virtually, in the view layer, rather than being implemented in a database schema.
- Fewer IT resources are required than for formal data structures (which require modeling).

Cons:

- As with the "Quick Wins" pattern, business users have to realize that they are working with raw operational data, whose quality is problematic and which may not be usable for all business applications.
- As with the "Quick Wins" pattern, data is not easily integrated with other data or reusable across the enterprise.
- Some IT work (to create data structures and ETL processes) is required.

Caveats:

1. Destination tables should be as flat (non-normalized) as possible to reduce complexity.

2. Perform only the minimal amount of data cleansing and transformation required at the table level.

3. Data should be accessed through a view layer, rather than by connecting to database tables.

4. Be aware that application data may not be suitable for all business needs and purposes.

5. As with the "Quick Wins" pattern, be careful when blending data sets from multiple sources together. Make sure the data has common or related business meanings and is joined on commonly-defined key attributes.

6. Begin creating and using metadata (more on this in a bit) to mitigate the risk and uncertainty of using operational data for BI purposes.

Note: This pattern is also sometimes referred to as the "Sandbox" pattern, wherein sets of data are copied to a local server for analysis by a single department or division. Sometimes, this data is used to support a single BI proof of concept

(POC) for that business unit. As with the previous Pattern, success is more likely if the department or division is using data it is familiar with, and if integration of data from multiple sources is kept to a minimum.

A single process improvement BI POC by one of our business divisions, using this pattern, netted $2 million in cost savings.

Pattern 3: Operational Data Store (ODS)

In this pattern, the organization begins the work of tying together current (or recent) data from multiple sources and integrating that data into a central repository on a database server or data appliance. This type of repository is called an Operational Data Store, or ODS.

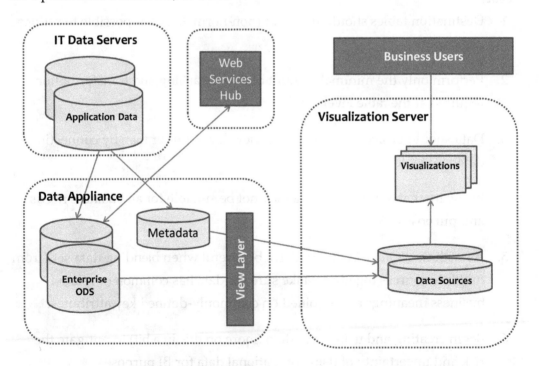

Ideally, this ODS should live on some sort of multi-processor parallel (MPP) data appliance, such as Teradata, Oracle Exadata, or Microsoft APS. The reason for this will be explained in more detail later, but essentially, we want to process very large amounts of data without having to put it into a rigidly defined format (e.g. a dimensional data structure) that has to be modified continually as business information needs change. The storage and processing capabilities of the data appliance allow us to store more historical data than would normally be feasible to store in an ODS, thus allowing the ODS, at least in the short term, to take on some of the capabilities of an enterprise data warehouse (EDW).

There are a number of similarities between an ODS and an enterprise data warehouse (EDW): data is designed around business subject areas, is stored at the most granular level of detail, and is organized in a more or less normalized fashion for quick and easy integration and reuse.

However, there are a number of important differences between an ODS and an EDW which must be noted:

1. In an EDW, data is made to conform to an agreed-upon semantic definition that is rigidly enforced. Data that doesn't conform to this definition is excluded from the EDW, even if it might be of importance to the business.

2. Data in an EDW is static and historical; it is updated via batch processes at scheduled intervals and is not updated in real time. An ODS must support real-time updating of data as well as scheduled batch updates when necessary.

3. An ODS usually does not contain any pre-calculated aggregations (summaries); any summarizations that are needed are calculated on the fly, from the detailed source records.

4. An EDW is read-only, and supports only reporting and BI/analytics use cases. An ODS can support the data needs of applications (including Cloud applications) and SOA web services, as well as BI and reporting uses.

5. An EDW consists of curated data, which requires a Data Governance structure and process to support it.

An ODS, then, enables us to begin realizing some of the benefits of an integrated, cross-organizational data store (e.g. reduction of the costs of supporting multiple redundant stores of inconsistent data, a more comprehensive view of enterprise data), while avoiding the cost and effort required by an EDW. An ODS also gives us more real-time data capabilities than an EDW does.

Use this pattern when:
- You want to begin the process of creating an integrated repository of enterprise-wide data, but need to do so iteratively.
- Data is cross-divisional in scope and needs to be provisioned for maximum reuse.
- Data from multiple sources needs to be integrated.
- You don't want to (or aren't ready to) create an EDW.
- You need to be able to work with data in motion (in real or near-real time), rather than data at rest.
- You want to be able to support applications and web services as well as BI and reporting.

Pros:
- Users and applications can see and work with data as it actually exists— not a sanitized version of data as we think it ought to exist.
- Users and applications have access to integrated data from multiple sources, in real or near-real time.
- An ODS can support applications and web services, as well as BI and reporting needs. This provides additional justification for the cost of the platform and data interfaces.
- Data can be more quickly and easily provisioned in response to new application or user requirements.
- Fewer IT resources are required than for an EDW.

Cons:
- Although data in an ODS is designed to conform more closely to business definitions (at least to the extent required to integrate multiple data sources), data values are not sanitized and may be different from what users expect.
- Requires some predefinition of data and schemas.

- Requires more IT involvement (schema creation, ETL, etc.) than previous patterns.

Caveats:

1. Data should be stored in a content-neutral form. Representations of data needed to support specific applications and semantic or informational viewpoints should be implemented in the view layer, rather than being implemented in a database schema. To improve performance, support these views at the database level using *join* and *aggregate* indexes as needed.

2. Store data at its most atomic level (i.e. not aggregated).

3. Data structures should be normalized enough to ensure reusability, but not over-normalized. Update performance is a minimal concern here.

4. Data should be represented in a form that is application-neutral and business-relevant.

5. Perform only the minimal amount of data cleansing and transformation required at the table level.

6. Implement the ODS iteratively, in response to application and BI requirements. Ensure that each iteration of the ODS delivers value to the business.

7. Do not allow ad-hoc updating of data in the ODS. Data updates should always be done in a controlled fashion, either through batch update processes or via web services.

8. Deprecate redundant data stores (such as those created in the "Quick Wins" and "Forklift" patterns) after data has been provisioned in the ODS.

PATTERN 4: DATA LAKE

In this pattern, the ODS is integrated with a "Data Lake" (Hadoop) platform that can accommodate unstructured and undefined (or less-defined) data, giving the organization the ability to analyze and respond to data in real or near-real time.

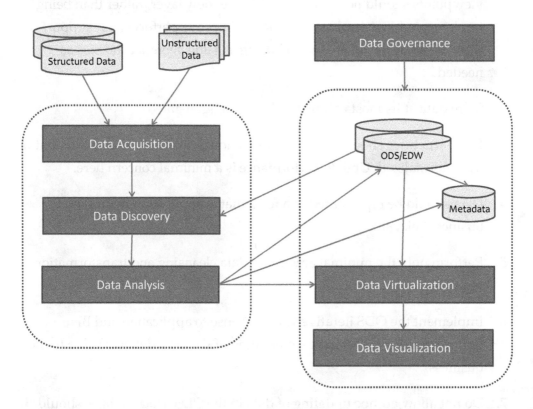

As data "mined" from the data lake is deemed useful for the enterprise, it can be structured and put into the ODS, or an EDW. Also, existing data in the ODS or EDW can be used to inform the process of analyzing new data that comes into the data lake environment, creating a positive feedback loop that leads more quickly to new insights. This environment supports real-time data analytics, known as Complex Event Processing or CEP. It also supports a governance process that helps create a more "data-driven" organization.

Use this pattern when:

- You want to begin the process of creating a data-driven organization.
- You want to be able to work with data that can't be predefined or pre-structured.
- Real-time data analytics are needed.

Pros:

- Supports unstructured as well as structured data.
- Allows data to be viewed, consumed, and manipulated in different ways.
- Supports data discovery as well as analytics.
- Supports complex event processing (CEP).
- Supports more mature BI processes (including data governance).

Cons:

- Requires the creation and management of BI and data governance processes.
- Requires implementation and understanding of more complex data and BI technology.

Caveats:

1. More specialized technical skills are required to use and support a "Data Lake" environment.

2. Processes must be created to govern the management of the data and the BI environment.

3. A closer collaboration between the business and IT is required.

4. The organization should be willing to become more "data driven," basing decisions on data analytics rather than "gut instinct."

These patterns are flexible, but I hope you get the point. You can't try to "eat the elephant" in BI. You must find a way to start from where you are, begin delivering value immediately to your customers and other business stakeholders, and then enlist their support for further BI initiatives. Each iteration develops your BI architecture and infrastructure further, helping you eat the elephant one bite at a time. Each iteration grows your BI knowledge and expertise, and improves your capability for delivering meaningful value to the business.

Key Points

- Patterns are very useful tools in Agile development. Patterns save time that would otherwise be spent "reinventing the wheel," support an iterative approach to development, and help deliver value quickly.

- A pattern-based approach to BI will help an organization gradually move:

    o   From application-defined data to business-defined data.

    o   From less integrated data to more integrated data.

    o   From less useful data to more useful data.

    o   From weaker BI capability to stronger BI capability.

    o   From more redundant data to less redundant data.

    o   From less IT involvement to more IT involvement.

    o   From less data governance to more data governance.

    o   From the current BI state to the target BI state.

- Patterns enable organizations to start from where they are, begin delivering value immediately to customers and other business stakeholders, and then enlist their support for further BI initiatives.

Chapter 8
"Working Toward"

The preceding chapter showed us several ways in which patterns can be used to gradually move an organization from a state of ad-hoc data and BI delivery to a target state architecture that supports:

- A more integrated, enterprise-wide view of data.
- Data that is more business-focused and less application-specific.
- Data that is multi-purposed instead of single-purposed.
- Real-time (or near real-time) data analytics.
- The ability to capture and analyze any data, in any form, anywhere.
- A more balanced collaboration between IT and the business.
- A more data-driven organization, with more data governance.
- A more capable and Agile organization.

It's important to realize that not only must this journey be taken in small and manageable steps, but that each step must lead, inexorably, to the desired destination. This is what Ann Lovejoy refers to in her book as "working toward."[25] Each piece of work, each technology investment, each lesson learned must begin by looking at the overall goal—not just the next step.

Lovejoy uses weeding as an example of this principle. Most of us have had the experience of spending an entire weekend weeding our garden, only to see all the weeds back in force the following weekend, leading to another weekend of weeding, and so on. Instead, Lovejoy advises, understand that what you're ultimately trying to do is not to weed the garden, but to make weeding the garden unnecessary! So, in small increments, weed a small section of the garden, mulch that section, and then cover the next section of the garden with plastic or newspapers (weighted down with rocks) or with "smother mulch" (mounds of wood chips, leaves, or straw). This will kill the weeds in that section of the garden and get it ready for mulching. Repeat this process one section of the garden at a time.

The point here is that each of our BI processes should not only identify a goal and move toward it, but also identify an obstacle and remove it. Each BI process we implement should not simply accomplish part of the work needed to move us toward our BI target state; it should do so in a way that makes further repetition of that work unnecessary (or at least faster and easier to do the next time).

As we cleanse data, we should put controls in place to make further cleansing of that data unnecessary. As we resolve each business question about data meaning, we should put a piece of data governance into place that forestalls future questions or concerns about that data. As we do the work of getting data into our data repository, we should automate and streamline the work of data integration so that it ceases to become such a time-consuming chore. By chipping away at the work of BI a small piece at a time, in a way that makes subsequent steps easier, we move toward our goal more quickly.

---

[25] Ibid, page 135.

In the next section, we'll go into more detail about things like data governance and metadata management. To close out this section, let's look at some "working toward" lessons we can learn from the pattern examples shown in the previous chapter:

1. An organization's technological capability needs to grow gradually, over time, to encompass increasingly complex BI technologies. Start with simple data visualization tools, then move on to data virtualization, data appliances, Hadoop, etc.

2. The quality, currency, and utility of an organization's data should gradually improve over time, both as data problems are identified and corrected (and as processes of data governance and master data management are gradually implemented) and as the organization's ability to work with non-static data (i.e. data in real time) develops.

3. Similarly, an organization's understanding of how to work with data also needs to grow over time. Companies must learn how to bridge the gap between what they know and what they need to know, and they must develop the ability to analyze data, challenge assumptions, recognize data and information that doesn't pass the "smell test,"[26] and create a culture of fact-based decision making. None of this happens overnight.

4. The division of responsibility between IT and the business will change and grow over time as well. In the beginning, the business' need for rapid results (and its inherent distrust of IT's competence) will necessitate an approach that gives IT less control over the data and BI delivery process than they might like. Over time, as the ability of IT to deliver BI value quickly to the business increases (along with the business' trust in IT), a more equal partnership will develop, with each performing those functions they are most suited for.

---

[26] That is, data that doesn't make sense in the context in which it is being used.

5.   The willingness of the business to support and fund BI initiatives, including ancillary data management and data governance processes, will increase over time as they realize the business benefits of this work. The business must see that there are quality issues with their data and inconsistencies in data values across organizational and functional boundaries. The business also needs to understand that these issues impact the business value returned from its BI initiatives. Only then will they appreciate the need for better quality data, more careful business definitions of data, more comprehensive metadata, and more robust data governance.

6.   Over time, our target-state BI architecture will work toward a balance of managed and unmanaged data, each supporting and reinforcing the other. Managed data supports "after the fact" analysis, and is used to inform the process of data discovery and the analysis of streaming (unmanaged) data. The results of this analysis can be structured and added to the store of managed data to inform subsequent analyses. Over time, this creates the store of knowledge that is needed to respond effectively, in real time, to data challenges and opportunities.

7.   Organizations will also, over time, develop the ability to seek out and work with data wherever it exists, in whatever form it's in. Don't limit yourself to data that can only be stored in a structured or relational form. Learn to work with text, picture, signal, event, and geolocation data as well. Continually seek out data that can challenge existing assumptions, not just validate them. Seek out data that can reveal problems and inefficiencies in existing business processes, and suggest new and better ways of doing things.

To flog a tired cliché: BI is a journey, not a destination. There are very few IT endeavors that attract more vendors and consultants promising "silver bullet" solutions and instant results. Organizations need to start with a realistic assessment of their data assets, technological capabilities, and cultural constraints, and then develop strategies for gradually enhancing their data management and BI/analytics capabilities.

By "working toward" your BI goals one piece at a time, you will inform each subsequent step of your BI journey with the lessons you have learned in previous steps. This will guarantee that your eventual destination will be not only the place you *intend* to be, but also the place you *need* to be.

Key Points

- An organization's BI architecture must grow, over time, to encompass several capabilities:

  - The ability to understand, make use of, and support increasingly complex data and BI technology.

  - An understanding of how to effectively manage data for maximum value.

  - The ability to work with data wherever it exists, in whatever form it's in, in real or near-real time.

  - The acceptance of fact-based, data-driven decision-making in the company's culture.

  - The ability to use data to drive value across and throughout the enterprise, including business process optimization and stakeholder management.

- BI processes must embody a "working toward" approach, which iteratively increases an organization's BI capabilities, identifies and removes obstacles and inefficiencies, and gradually moves the business toward its desired BI target state.

- By informing each step of the BI journey with lessons learned from previous steps, the ultimate target state will be what the business actually needs, not just what IT thinks it needs.

After creating the design of the landscape, and establishing the "hardscape" that defines the "bones" of the garden, the next step is to create the garden itself. In gardening, you start from the soil, and work your way up: humus, ground cover, grasses, plants and flowers, shrubs and trees. In BI, you start from the data and—most importantly—the metadata, which helps you manage the risks and opportunities of using the data.

In this section, we'll start from the basic design of the BI architecture, and discuss various ways of creating the BI infrastructure. We will also address the problem of how to reconcile IT-based data management processes with business-based BI processes.

Remember that, as we've noted before, there is no "one size fits all" solution for BI in any given organization, any more than there is a "one size fits all" implementation of a garden. Take what's written here with the appropriate measure of salt. Use the material in this section as a jumping-off point for discussions with your stakeholders about the most effective ways to begin implementing BI in your company.

Chapter 9
Data and Dirt

As Ann Lovejoy writes, "Good gardens begin with great soil." But great soil—even good soil—is rare in most parts of the country. Rarer still is an understanding of what constitutes great soil, and of how to turn native dirt (mostly sand, clay, and rock) into great soil.

There is an entire branch of botany, called *soil science*, dedicated to fostering an understanding of the importance and characteristics of great soil. Soil science tells us, for example, that the problem with most dirt is not a lack of nutrients, but a lack of the soil microorganisms that convert these nutrients into forms that plants can consume. It tells us that more plants are lost to poor water drainage than to poor nutrition. And it tells us that many, if not most, of our current gardening and fertilizing practices are actually *harmful* to soil microorganisms, and thus to plants.

Similarly, successful BI initiatives begin with good data. But just as most gardeners lack an understanding of soil science, so do most BI practitioners lack an understanding of the discipline called "data management"[27] (or data resource management). Data management, if properly carried out, would show practitioners how to transform raw operational (i.e. application) data into data suitable for BI.

Most companies don't perform data management, for the same reasons that most gardeners don't practice soil science. They may lack an understanding of its importance, or be overwhelmed by its apparent complexity, or simply not want to spend time and effort on it. All they want are the results—*right now!* So amateur gardeners will till or double-dig the soil (which brings poor soil up to the surface and buries living topsoil underground), shove in some plants and shrubs, and then add chemical fertilizers, inadvertently killing off the remaining soil microorganisms and making the plants completely dependent on the fertilizer, which must be continually replenished.

In the same way, companies trying to perform BI will often adopt a "rip and run" approach, dumping raw operational data onto a BI platform (e.g. Hadoop, SAP's HANA, Tableau, QlikView) or a data appliance (e.g. Teradata, Oracle's Exadata, Microsoft's APS), then connecting to that data with some sort of data visualization or analytics tool (e.g. Tableau, SAP's Lumira, Microsoft Power BI). Bad data, if and when discovered, is masked somewhere in the ETL process. Finally, it's left up to the individual business user to work around the data problems in their visualization tool.

In gardening, the advantages of having good soil are many. You get much healthier plants, more beautiful flowers, and tastier vegetables. You reduce the risk of unexpected plant deaths due to poor nutrition and poor drainage. And, most importantly, you create a *sustainable* garden: a garden that requires less time, effort, and expense with each passing year. A sustainable garden is a garden that keeps itself healthy, disease-free, and well-nurtured.

---

[27] This is not the same thing as what is now being called "data science", which refers to the pattern analysis of data. What many so-called "data scientists" don't know about data would fill a book. Like this one.

Good data, like good soil, confers similar benefits to a BI environment. Business users don't have to spend abundant time and effort questioning the data, validating the data, or cleansing the data. There is less risk that multiple users will cleanse or transform the same data differently, leading to different results. Reports and analyses created from the data will be more trustworthy. The data will be more reusable, and more valid across organizational or functional boundaries. And, as with gardens, a BI environment built on good data will be more sustainable, not requiring continual effort and expense to maintain.

DATA MANAGEMENT MISCONCEPTIONS

This, of course, begs an obvious question: since having good data is so important to successful BI initiatives, why don't more companies follow good data management practices? I think there are three misconceptions about data quality that have taken root in the thinking of business managers, causing them to view data management efforts with distrust and suspicion. These misconceptions need to be confronted and addressed before any progress in this area can be made:

- **Misconception #1: Data quality is "all or nothing."** Unfortunately, too many data practitioners take an absolutist approach to data management, viewing data quality as some sort of idealized notion of data purity. In asset management (recall from the first section that we are regarding data as a business asset), a risk management approach is taken: how may the asset best be used, at the least cost and the lowest risk? If risks exist, how may they be most effectively mitigated? This is the approach that needs to be taken with the management of data. Data does not have to be perfect, but the risks of using data in any form need to be understood, and mitigated where appropriate. As we shall see in a later chapter, this is where the concept of *metadata* becomes important.

- **Misconception #2: All data quality issues must be resolved before any of the data can be used.** This misconception is especially troubling, not only because the rapid pace of today's business world necessitates an equally rapid processing and understanding of data, but also because, in many cases, the exact nature, characteristics, and value of a company's data can't be understood in advance. There is a symbiotic relationship between the analysis of data and our understanding of it; to say that data can't be analyzed until it is fully understood rejects the very means that often must be used to understand it! Again, this becomes a risk management issue: we don't have to know enough to trust the data completely, but we need to know whether we can trust it enough to use it for a given business purpose.

- **Misconception #3: Data quality depends on a single semantic understanding of the data.** This, I think, is one of the more dangerous misconceptions, and one on which the whole notion of "data warehousing" is based. This is why, in my company and in many other companies, the term "data warehousing" is rarely even mentioned. Of all the problems that must be overcome in a traditional approach to data warehousing, the most intractable one is trying to get a company's entire management structure to agree on common definitions of business terms, and a common understanding of business processes. Once reached (if ever), this common understanding is encapsulated in the schema of the data warehouse, which means that as this understanding changes (and it always will), the schema of the data warehouse must be continually refactored to reflect the new understanding. What is most essentially needed in BI, I think, is not a "single version of the truth," but a single trusted and integrated store of data that can support multiple semantic "views of the truth" and multiple organizational information needs, in a form that can be quickly and easily modified as business semantics and information needs change.

In gardening, you begin with the understanding that your soil is imperfect, and needs to be improved. Most of the time, we don't know exactly how, or to what extent, our soil needs to be improved. And, most of the time, we need to find a way to create landscapes and gardens without perfect soil. So we perform tests (like soil acidity tests and biotic counts) to identify our soil needs, we perform the minimal amount of soil amendment needed to get our garden established, we identify the biggest risks (like poor drainage) and pests (like soil pathogens), and we take initial steps to address these problem areas.

Over time, we work to break down soil into humus, improve soil drainage, increase the number of healthy soil microorganisms, and suppress harmful pathogens. The goal is to create a garden that nurtures plants and keeps weeds and pests at bay without requiring the use of artificial fertilizers and pesticides. We also put in place a *process* of soil management, in which the detritus of garden and food waste is composted and fed back into the soil in an endless cycle of sustainability.

Similarly, in BI we almost never get to start with perfect data, so we need to figure out what we can do with the data we currently have, what we need to do in order to make the data good enough for the purposes we want to achieve, and finally, over time, put into place a process of data management that feeds well-understood and business-trusted data into our BI environment, in a way that doesn't require legions of IT workers and weeks of time to achieve.

This vision of data sustainability is called *data governance*: the management of business data by business users for business purposes, in a way that doesn't require constant and expensive intervention by IT support. In gardening terms, it's the creation of a landscape you can take care of yourself, without having to hire a gardening service and groundskeepers.

SOME INCONVENIENT TRUTHS

So how do we get to "trustworthy data" (not "perfect data")? Let's start by acknowledging some "inconvenient truths" about bad data:

1. It's not bad data (which is to say, incorrect data values) that will hurt you. It's bad data that you *don't know* is bad. In other words, data that you think is correct, but isn't; data that you think means one thing but that actually means something different. To put this another way, the essential data

problem isn't data *quality* per se, but rather data *transparency*. Business users are accustomed to working with bad data (usually in MS Excel or Access); they know how to recognize bad data when they see it at the record level, and either correct it or filter it out. The danger occurs when more automated BI and analytics processes make assumptions about the data that may turn out not to be valid. Case in point: the 2008 mortgage derivatives fiasco that triggered a global recession!

2. There is often, as Wayne Kernochan puts it, "more information in bad data than good data." For example, one of the things we want to achieve with BI is to use data to identify problems or inefficiencies in business processes. These problems usually manifest themselves as bad (or unexpected) data values. If we pre-sanitize our data to conform to expected values before we let our users see it, we're effectively shielding them from the very information that would help them identify and fix business problems, or recognize opportunities for improvement! At the same time, we want to be sure our users recognize these data values as anomalies and respond to them appropriately (i.e., we don't want them to assume that these are normal, to-be-expected data values). Again, the issue here is data transparency, not data quality.

3. Data quality is contextual. This harkens back to a phenomenon I describe as "The Ugly Truth About Data Quality." Data that works perfectly well in one context (for example, supporting a single IT application) becomes woefully deficient when shifted into a different context (a data warehouse, let's say). Back when I was doing data warehousing, application developers used to just stare at me when I told them how bad their data was. "But the application isn't blowing up!" they'd say, "What's the problem?" The problem is that what works perfectly well for one purpose fails miserably when used for another.

4. Business users (especially the ones who hold the purse strings) are not going to spend money on data quality, data governance, master data management, etc., unless they can see for themselves the probable

consequences and potential business risk of inadequately managed data. It's the classic chicken-and-egg problem: we can't fix our company's data without an investment of time, money and resources, which we can't receive until our company understands the consequences of *not* fixing the data!

I hope you see where I'm going with this. What business users need is not "perfect data," but data about which they have enough information to know what they can and can't use it for, with minimum risk. In other words, what they need is not perfect data, but adequate *metadata*. Metadata helps us create a data (and BI) environment that doesn't shield business users from bad data, but keeps them from shooting themselves in the foot with it.

MEANING OF METADATA

Let me explain, first off, what I mean by *metadata*. To most people, it means "data about data," which is probably the single most unhelpful definition of anything I've ever heard. Most vendors define metadata in terms of *lineage*: the documenting of data sources, integrations, and transformations. This gets us somewhat closer, but is still lacking. I define metadata in terms of a single question: What does a business user need to know in order to use a given set of data safely and profitably?

Here are some of the things that business users need to know about their data:

1. What business process(es) created the data? It doesn't help to tell users that a given set of data came from Application A or from Database D. They need to know what business process or department created the data.

2. What is the purpose for which the data was created, and what is its intended use?

3. What are the expected normal values, or range of values, for this data?

4. What outliers (non-normal data values) have been identified for this data?

5. How current is this data? How often is it updated?

6. At what point is the data considered "out of date," and should therefore not be relied upon?

7. Who is allowed to view or use this data? Who is allowed to update it? Who, specifically, should *not* be allowed to view or update it?

8. Who, if anyone, audits or reviews this data for correctness?

9. What computations, integrations, transformations and/or derivations were involved in the creation of this data? What is/was the business justification for them?

10. For what business purposes is it appropriate to use this data? For what business purposes is it *not* appropriate? For example, data that may safely be used to create a monthly balance sheet for one department may be considered inadequate for, say, a regulatory audit.

Here's a gardening example of what I mean by metadata: have you ever bought a soaker hose for your garden? Did you place it on the ground next to your plants? Wrong! You're supposed to bury it under at least 3 or 4 inches of mulch. The purpose of a soaker hose is not to water the plants, it's to moisten the mulch! When you use it the right way, it keeps your plants alive with much less water; when you use it the wrong way, most of the water evaporates into the air and never reaches the plants.

Unfortunately, though, the soaker hose rarely comes with any information that tells you how to properly use it! The soaker hose is missing metadata— information that tells you how (and how not) to use it in a way that delivers maximum value while avoiding pitfalls. Adequate metadata about your data will help you in the same way.

Where does this metadata come from? Generally speaking, metadata is generated while working with business users to identify the most appropriate sources of data needed to support a particular BI function or application, and creating the ETL (or similar) processes need to get this data onto a platform that can be easily used.

Some of the information (e.g. the expected and outlier values) can only come from searching through the data with queries, or using a data profiling tool. Some will come from business users themselves, or from company management (e.g. the records retention department, if your company has one), or from one or more data governance stewards (again, if your company has a data governance structure and process). You won't necessarily be able to get *all* of the above information for every set of data. But the more you can inform your users about the data they are using, the less likely they will be to get themselves into trouble.

How should this information be published and disseminated? Again, it depends on both the technological and organizational maturity of your company. It might be something as simple as a spreadsheet that is periodically updated and posted to either a common file share or something like a MS SharePoint site. If you have a data appliance, data warehouse or ODS, you can create a set of query-friendly tables (with one or more covering views) in the database. There are metadata management products in the marketplace that can help with this effort. What's important is that this information must be easily accessible to all users, and that there is a defined and controlled process for keeping it accurate and up to date.

"NON-INVASIVE" APPROACH TO DATA QUALITY

As noted above, BI data stores present data quality challenges that application databases don't have. For one thing, you can precisely define data values for an application database, but you probably shouldn't try to define them for a BI database. As previously mentioned, there may be crucial information in "incorrect" data values that need to be revealed to the business.

On the other hand, you also want to minimize the adverse impact that incorrect or unexpected data values might have on analyses of data, and decisions thereby made. What is needed here is a mechanism for defining expected values (i.e. the domain) for a data attribute and for detecting and reporting exceptions (i.e. domain outliers) to the appropriate data stewards.

Here's an approach that I've used successfully in the past: for each data attribute, I create a regex (regular expression) validator for the data. For example, for an automobile license plate number whose expected values are of the form ABC1234 (i.e. exactly three capital letters followed by exactly four numbers), the regex validator looks like this:

[A-Z]{3}[0-9]{4}

I also define an indicator that denotes the attribute as being either optional or required. Then I create a batch process that periodically vets the actual data against the expected range of values. When unexpected values are found, a record is written to an exception table in the database. This table is connected to an online report (using something like SQL Reporting Services). Each morning, business users and data stewards can look at the report to determine whether data anomalies that need to be corrected have surfaced. They can follow up with the creators or updaters of the data to get the data problem fixed.

Another approach (one that's often used with NoSQL databases) is to codify the business data rules into an application or script that can be periodically run against the data. Again, the output from this process must be fed into some type of reporting environment in order to bring data anomalies to the attention of people who can fix them.

This gives business users the best of both worlds: they can see the data that actually exists (not just the data that IT allows them to see), and they can identify and fix problematic data before it's used for reporting and analysis.

In the same way that soil microorganisms convert soil nutrients into a consumable form for plants, metadata helps convert raw data into a form that's safe for our business to use.

Key Points

- As soil is the raw material of gardening, so is data the raw material of BI.

- As in gardening, the soil (data) doesn't have to be perfect to start out; it can be good enough for some purposes and then improved over time.

- Data profiling, like soil testing, helps show us where our data can be improved.

- Creating and publishing business-focused metadata helps reduce the risk of using imperfect data for BI purposes.

- Data transparency is more important than data quality. It's not bad data that hurts you; it's bad data you don't know about!

Chapter 10
A Room With Many Views

L andscapes are built around the concept of *rooms*. As previously mentioned, different parts of the garden perform different functions: some are used for entertaining, some are used for play, some are used for meditation, and so on. The trick is to tie these different areas together into a unified and easily accessible whole, while still retaining their individual characteristics and function.

We usually accomplish this using a combination of *screenings* and *focal points*. Screenings are things like large shrubs, small hedges, or fences that shield one part of the garden from the view of another. Focal points are things like ornamental ponds, garden art, or statues that catch and hold the eye. And, of course, we use paths and grassy areas to guide people through each room of the garden, while also providing ample seating and resting areas for rest and meditation.

What we want to accomplish in our BI environment is something very similar to this. We want to give our customers the view of the garden, and the garden experience, that best meets their individual needs—without having to create an individual garden for each one of them. Even if we *could* create an individual garden for each person, it still wouldn't work. What each person needs from the garden will vary from day to day: people will feel energetic and extroverted one day, meditative and introspective the next. So a well-designed garden (and BI environment) will give people what they need at any given moment.

The problem with most BI environments (dimensional data marts are a great example) is that they are created for a single purpose, and they can't be made to fulfill any other purpose without a large amount of effort and cost. Most BI environments today are like English cottage gardens: no matter where you go in the garden, the experience is always exactly the same!

What we need is a data and BI environment that adapts quickly and easily to the data needs of each individual user, providing each person with the representation of the data needed to achieve a particular business purpose. And we need to be able to create and change these representations quickly and easily, with a minimum of cost, effort, and IT intervention.

What's needed in our BI garden are *information views:* abstractions or virtualizations of data that work like rooms in a garden landscape. They will screen some parts of the data from view while focusing attention on others. In doing so, they will enable us to create different data experiences for our customers, in the same way that landscape rooms create different experiences in the garden.

This is, in my opinion, one of the hardest data problems to solve, and one which elicits the greatest amount of disagreement and contention among data professionals. How do you create a data environment that is both cohesive (in that the data is integrated meaningfully and defined in business terms) and differentiated (so that end users aren't shoehorned into a single view of data)? What characteristic properties of data need to be enforced at the schema (or storage) level, and which can safely and profitably be differentiated at some higher level of abstraction?

The Problem of Over-Consolidation

Remember my earlier story about building the deck? I used this story to illustrate two important points: focus on managing the most important risks, and defer as much work as possible to the point where it's actually needed. What we learned from the Data Federation fiasco in the early 2000s was that data quality problems manifest themselves at the point where different sets of data are integrated together. In my company, for example, two different parts from two different divisions can have the same part number; conversely, two of the same part from different divisions can have different part numbers. So, at the schema (or storage) level, the risk you most need to mitigate is the risk of what I call *over-consolidation:* bringing different things together and treating them as though they were the same thing.

When we began building our ODS (operational data store), the platform vendor sent out a consultant who created a provisional data model for us. When I looked at the data model, I saw a single entity for Part (called "Item"), but it was involved in relationships with entities associated with different business processes (design, engineering, manufacturing, aftersales). Moreover, most of the attributes in the Item entity were nullable (optional). What this told me was that a bunch of different things had been conglomerated together into one thing, and that we were going to have a serious problem moving forward with this design! I broke out the Item entity into a set of Item subtypes (Manufacturing Item, Purchasing Item, Aftersales Item, etc.), so that each subtype could have its own attributes and participate in meaningful associations with appropriate other entities.

At the schema (or storage) level, you clearly must be very careful about creating "conformed" entities: entities in which data from different sources are merged together and given a common name and business meaning. There are many occasions where this can be done safely; there are other occasions where doing this can get you into serious trouble.

It's important to ask a lot of questions of business subject matter experts to determine when and how data can be meaningfully integrated together. When it can't, or when a determination can't be made, the safest course is to create additional entities and attributes and give them differentiated names and definitions. If the same entity or attribute has different meanings in different areas of your company, then create multiple entities and attributes in your data store, named and defined in a way that denotes the source, business meaning, and the characteristics that make each entity different from similar entities or attributes in other data sources (also called "differentiations"). Instead of a single *Customer* entity and *Customer Begin Date* attribute, for example, you'll likely have multiple entities for *Purchase Customer*, *Lease Customer*, *Warranty Customer*, *Aftersales Customer*, etc., with corresponding differentiations in attributes.

Similarly, not all data quality issues need to be addressed at the schema (storage) level—only the most significant ones. For example, in moving data from an Oracle database into our data store, I discovered duplicate primary key values. In Oracle, trailing blanks are not truncated, so '12345' and '12345<*blank*>' are treated as two separate values. In our target ODS, trailing blanks *are* truncated, so these two key values became identical. I took this issue back to our business customers for a resolution; they changed the key values in the source application. The problem with duplicate part numbers across our different operating divisions was addressed by making *Division Code* and *Part Number* a compound key.

Having dealt with the major risks associated with bringing data from multiple sources into a common data store, we are free to defer the work of resolving other data issues to a more opportune time. Most of these are data governance issues that need to be discussed and resolved by the business. For example, now that the issue of duplicate and inconsistent part numbers has been revealed, our business divisions are discussing how to resolve this problem. But we are *not* holding up the work of making part data available to the business until we are able to create a single conformed part entity!

Note the importance of involving the business in the work of creating the integrated data store. Too often, IT makes the mistake of trying to solve these problems based on assumptions that may not be valid. For example, an IT person might have tried to solve the duplicate key problem described above by simply dropping the "duplicate" record. This would have been a mistake, as the records referred to two completely different business transactions! Similarly, an IT person might assume that two fields (in two different databases) with the same name mean the same thing; these assumptions need to be validated by the business.

In my company, for example, the data field *Actual Delivery Date* can have different meanings in the context of different business processes. The Agile solution to this problem is not to try to create a single conformed *Actual Delivery Date* field (unless this can be done quickly and easily); it's to create as many precisely defined variants of *Actual Delivery Date* as are needed to support the different business definitions, and then give each business unit an information view in which *Actual Delivery Date* is mapped to the appropriate attribute.

THE PROBLEM OF UNDER-CONSOLIDATION

This approach begs a question: how do we eventually reconcile all (or at least some) of these competing and contradictory data viewpoints? This is the opposite problem of the one described above. If we know that (or aren't sure whether) A and B are two different things, they need to be kept separate at the schema (storage) level. But if we find out later that they are, in fact, the same thing, how do we make them the same?

This is fundamentally a data governance question, and it's one that information views can help with. If we have sufficiently exposed our metadata to the business so as to inform them that there exist similar attributes A and B with different business definitions, the business can decide whether these attributes should be combined into a single business concept. Once that decision has been reached, the database schema and metadata can be refactored, and the associated information views can be changed to point to the newly redefined attribute. At the information view layer, the name and type of the attribute remain unchanged; they just point to a different column in the database. User applications (including data visualizations) are not impacted, and don't need to change.

The process we've described can be summarized as follows:

1. Get data into the repository as quickly as possible, with just enough definition to ensure that entities and attributes have distinct business meanings and are not redundant.

2. Cover the data in the repository with information views that give each business unit the representation of the data they need. Require that *all* access to data in the repository use these views.

3. Publish metadata that accurately describes the data behind each information view: where it comes from, what it means, what values should be expected, how current it is, etc.

4. Create a data governance process that allows business users to discuss and resolve differences in data meaning and issues with data quality, using the metadata as input to these discussions.

5. Create a data management process that implements these business decisions by refactoring the data model, data store, and information views iteratively as required.

By taking this approach, we avoid two common BI mistakes: waiting too long to deliver data (and value) to the business, and allowing data to proliferate into redundant silos inside of specific business units.

THE VALUE OF INFORMATION VIEWS

As we've seen, the information views play an important part in enabling an Agile approach to BI.

- Views enable the storage of data to be content-neutral. By storing only data structures (which don't often change) at the schema level and putting semantic meaning and informational content (which change more frequently) into views, you can avoid the pain of having to refactor database schemas whenever business meaning or information needs change.

- Data can be stored at its most atomic level and aggregated in the view layer. If performance is an issue, support these views at the database level with *join* and/or *aggregate* indexes as needed, or materialize the views.

- Application data can be represented in a more business-meaningful form. This is important when giving business users access to raw operational data (as in the "Quick Wins" and "Forklift" patterns); data in application databases is often incomprehensible to business users.

- Data from different table sources can be integrated together into a more meaningful and cohesive whole, thus simplifying user queries and making the data more useable.

- Views insulate business users from the impact of schema changes. As we saw with the "Forklift" pattern, information views can be repointed from the Forklift (staging/landing pad) tables to the ODS without impacting existing data visualizations and end-user queries.

- Views can be used to mask or cleanse bad data values (be careful about doing this, though, and do so only after consultation with the business).

- Views can help enforce security requirements and control access to data where necessary.

The use of information views helps us avoid a third common BI mistake: creating BI data structures that have to be refactored every time business meanings or information needs change (as, for example, with dimensional data marts!).

Key Points

- When designing the data repository for a BI solution, avoid the counterpart mistakes of *over-consolidation* (treating different attributes as though they were the same) and *under-consolidation* (allowing a proliferation of redundant attributes).

- At the schema (or storage) level, implement data in an atomic and content-neutral form, with a minimum of data cleansing and transformation.

- Use *information views* to ascribe semantic meaning and information value to data. Views can be refactored quickly and easily as information needs change; database schemas cannot.

- Use a data governance process to review the data in your BI repository (based on the published metadata) and recommend data consolidations as needed. These consolidations will require schema changes to the database, but the impact of these changes will be masked by the information views.

- Views can also simplify queries, integrate data from different sources, enforce security and access requirements, and improve performance.

Chapter 11
Perennial BI

A side from trees and shrubs, which are used for many foundational purposes, the stalwarts of the garden are annual and perennial plants. As the names suggest, annuals bloom for a season and then die, whereas perennials will last for years or even decades. Some perennials are evergreen, and others die back each year and then regenerate in the spring from seeds or a dormant crown. Perennials give the garden its year-round shape, composition, and texture, though they may only bloom for a short time each year.

Annuals are the "quick win" plants — the ones you use when you need to fill a pot, container, or bed with immediate color and texture. All you need is some planting mix and an occasional shot of fertilizer or plant food. Annuals are often used to "fill in" a new garden while waiting for more permanent plants to become established. They require little if any maintenance. However, the color and appearance of annuals is static and unchanging; they perform one function and one function only. A marigold is a marigold is a marigold. Furthermore, the gardener incurs the expense of replacing these plants year after year after year; basing a garden on annuals is a good way to go broke!

Perennials are the workhorses of the garden, satisfying many year-round needs. To quote Ann Lovejoy, "Perennials are the lifeblood of the garden, providing the pulsing flow of color and change that enlivens the relatively static framework of woody plants."[28] Perennials can serve many different purposes in the garden, and can be adapted to any need. They blend all the other elements of the garden (the hardscape, trees, shrubs, and other garden features) together into a cohesive whole. However, they need more careful attention (including mulching, fertilizing, and pruning); perennials depend on a steady intake of nutrients, and require much more maintenance than annuals.

Trees and woody shrubs provide the backbone of the garden, but are relatively monolithic; their appearance rarely changes. Here in the Pacific Northwest, it's common for gardeners to plant most of their property with rhododendrons and azaleas, which bloom for perhaps two weeks in mid-to-late spring and look as dull as dishwater for the remainder of the year. I tend to think of data warehouses and "data vaults" as the rhododendrons of BI: they underpin and support the BI effort, and occasionally provide a flourish of value, but most of the time they just sit there.

Annuals are like all the "one-offs" of BI — the endless proliferation of data dumps, spreadmarts, localized data marts, and other tools used to meet immediate BI needs, enlist support for BI initiatives, provide training in BI tools, or (just as with annuals in the garden) act as a stop-gap while a more robust BI architecture is being put into place. They provide immediate short-term value, but don't really contribute much to a cohesive, strategic, long-term BI architecture. And, as with annuals, the cost of sustaining an enterprise-wide BI strategy based on a proliferation of disconnected point solutions will be prohibitively expensive.

---

[28] Ibid, page 273.

What Is "Perennial BI"?

What we need in our organizations is what I've taken to calling "Perennial BI": an approach that makes use of data sources (such as data warehouses and data vaults) without being bound or constrained by them, that supports short-term BI initiatives without making them the focus of the BI architecture, that pulls all the elements of the BI infrastructure together into a cohesive whole, and that is infinitely adaptable in response to changing needs and conditions.

Perennials in the garden are used primarily for *composition*—they provide a variety of sizes, colors, and textures that can be combined to produce different effects and meet different gardening needs. The use of perennials in the garden is analogous to the use of light and shadow in painting; the intent is to draw the viewer's eye here, or invoke a mood there. Perennials are continually changing color and shape. They can often bloom multiple times, at different times of the year, and even their leaves can change color throughout the seasons!

In order to use perennials effectively in the garden, one must make a fundamental shift in thinking: the garden must no longer be viewed as a static aggregation of plant and landscape objects combined into a monolithic whole. Instead, the garden must be viewed as a continually changing mobile of colors, shapes, and moods that meet different needs (e.g. inspiration, meditation, reassurance, play) in different ways throughout the year.

This is analogous to the fundamental shift in thinking we must make in BI: to put the emphasis of our BI architecture on *data in motion*, not data at rest. Or, to put this another way, to shift the focus of BI from *insight* to *action*.

From Insight to Action

Traditionally, the purpose of BI and analytics was to promote *insight*: the derivation of causes, effects, and implications from a defined set of static data. This was the premise upon which data warehousing, data marts, data vaults, and similar initiatives were based.[29] Most organizations' BI architecture became the IT equivalent of the English cottage garden—you couldn't really do anything in it, all you could do was look at it.

Now, with the advent of predictive, prescriptive, and preventative analytics, the emphasis of BI is becoming less about knowing and more about doing. BI has become, in gardening terms, more like the "outdoor living room" or patio entertainment area—it's about what you can *do* with the space, not how it looks. The focus of BI has shifted from "what does this mean?" to "how do we respond to this?"

This means that it's no longer enough to have a repository of static data, however well-defined and cleansed. What we need now is the ability to understand (in real or near-real time) the meaning or significance of streams of data—not completely, but just enough to know what action(s) need to be taken in response to that data. Our BI data stores need to do much more than simply support static analyses, visualizations and dashboards; they need to support day-to-day and moment-by-moment operational activities and decision-making.

Our BI architecture also needs to be *adaptable*, in ways that traditional BI architecture hasn't been. It needs to be able to support the movement, integration, consumption, and use of data in all forms, for all purposes, in all places and at all times. IT has traditionally tried to provision this sort of adaptability through the use of data replication. IT will take data from the mainframe, for example, and copy it to a SQL database to make it more accessible for operational reporting. Then they'll replicate it to a NoSQL database in support of SOA web services, and then replicate it again to Hadoop to support predictive analytics.

The same data may be replicated to multiple data marts to support the specific operational or decision-making needs of different organizational areas. It is often *localized:* combined with local data or defined in semantically different terms to make it more relevant or usable for a particular business unit. And, with each

---

[29] These days, if I'm asked whether I favor Inmon or Kimball, I'm likely to answer "No".

replication, the cost of data goes up, the ROI of data goes down, the difficulty and expense of maintaining the BI infrastructure increases, and so does the risk of organizational failure resulting from disparate, disintegrated, and inconsistent data.

CHARACTERISTICS OF PERENNIAL BI

So how do we implement this vision of "Perennial BI," and what does it look like? I hesitate to be too prescriptive here, because every organization's BI needs (like every garden) are different. But here are some basic and important concepts that you will see reiterated throughout this book:

- **Separate information from data.** The rocky shoal upon which many BI initiatives run aground is an insistence on defining data in terms of specific information requirements. These information requirements become baked into the definition of the database schema (or document schema, if a NoSQL database is being used), requiring that the schemas be continually refactored in response to ever-changing information needs and requirements. As mentioned above, we want to keep the storage of data informationally and semantically neutral, and add content as needed at the time of provisioning.

- **Abstract the consumption of data from the storage of data.** The use of data abstraction techniques that I describe in my book *Building the Agile Database*[30] becomes an especially important consideration in BI. Database views, web services, and data virtualization portals are vital tools that enable real-time provisioning of integrated, semantically-tailored, information-enriched, consumer-specific sets of data. Furthermore, they do so in ways that don't require constant refactoring of database and document schemas, creation of database linkages, modification of ETL processes, and more general hassle. Abstracting the delivery of data

---

[30] Burns, Larry. *Building the Agile Database*. Technics Publications (N.J.), 2011.

provides a layer of insulation between the data and the consumer, so that changes in the schema don't adversely impact data consumers, and changes in information requirements don't require constant refactoring of the database.

- **Keep data in motion as often as possible, and at rest as seldom as possible.** One way of doing this is to make your BI data store/infrastructure the datacenter of a Service-Oriented Architecture (SOA) web services hub. Use web services, operating along an enterprise service bus (ESB), to keep data in your data store flowing to and from a variety of applications and other data producers and consumers. Make data quickly and easily available to any authorized consumer, for any valid organizational purpose.

- **Share data and information across the organization.** According to a Geckoboard survey of 250 owners of small and medium-sized businesses across the U.S.,[31] business success (defined as meeting some or all organizational goals) is predicated on: a) tracking metrics against defined organizational KPIs in real time, and b) transparently sharing the results of these metrics with company stakeholders in real time. According to the study, 50% of companies who track and share metrics in real time meet all their organizational goals, compared with 24% who don't.

- **Seek out the data you don't know you need.** Wayne Kernochan[32] makes the excellent point that in traditional BI, we tend to focus our attention on the data we assume we need, while ignoring (or not proactively looking for) data that might challenge those assumptions. He cites as an example the 2008 mortgage derivatives meltdown: the financial models that allowed Wall Street firms to profit from mortgage debt failed to seek out data that

---

[31] Stares, Lindsay. "Small Businesses Report Benefits of Real-Time Data." TDWI, June 1, 2016. http://bit.ly/2a53XNi.

[32] Kernochan, Wayne. Op. cit.

would challenge or validate the assumptions upon which the models were based. There is business value in using data to better support customers in an existing market, but limiting yourself to that data leads to what marketing theory calls *marketing myopia:* failure to realize that you should be in a different market! Kernochan asserts that a truly Agile approach to BI requires proactively searching out data that challenges our assumptions about the data we think we need.

- **Focus on improving operations, not analysis.** BI delivers the greatest value when information is used at the operational level, to improve quality, streamline business processes, improve stakeholder relationships, and support new product development, as opposed to improving static decision-making (say, by creating a nifty dashboard for the CEO). You get more bang for your BI buck when information and analysis is delivered directly to front-line workers, rather than to back-office decision-makers.

EXAMPLES OF PERENNIAL BI

Let's look at some real-life examples of "Perennial BI" in action:

- **Groupon:** Groupon uses big data analysis of its website activities to create and manage its customer master data. This enables Groupon to target its customers with specific products and services, using applications such as its new GrouponNow service.[33]

- **UPS:** UPS uses big data to manage relationships with its customers, through a service called "UPS My Choice." For $40 per year, customers can create a customized delivery plan with delivery dates, times, and locations,

---

[33] Boyd, E. B. Interview with LinkedIn's Reid Hoffman on Groupon's Big Advantage: Big Data. Fast Company, November 18, 2011: http://bit.ly/2a04m8m.

security codes, alternate delivery locations, and more. So far, more than 2 million customers have signed up for this service.[34]

- **Express Scripts**: Express Scripts, an online prescription drug provider, analyzes over 1 billion pharmacy insurance claims annually, feeding the results of their analyses to a process improvement team. Potential customers are identified and contacted with information about how they can save money by using Express Scripts' online ordering system instead of filling prescriptions at a pharmacy. Express Scripts' "ExpressPath" service portal, which enables customers to manage their prescriptions online, has over 3 million customers. Average savings on prescriptions is 10-15%; approval times have been reduced from 72 hours to 12 hours.[35]

- **Intel:** Intel uses predictive analytics to identify which potentially high-volume resellers it should focus its sales efforts on. This has increased sales by $20 million in the Asia-Pacific region alone. Predictive analytics are also used to reduce product testing time, with savings expected to top $30 million.[36]

- **Dannon:** The dairy giant formerly relied on Excel spreadsheets to forecast sales and manage inventory. Using predictive analytics, they can now accurately predict the outcome of a marketing promotion and its effect on sales. Since Dannon's adoption of big data in 2011, accuracy of sales forecasting and inventory planning has increased from about 70% to 98%, and its market share has increased from 2.8% in 2011 to nearly 13% in 2012. Dannon also uses predictive analytics to forecast the results of price cuts and product mixes in different parts of the country. This allows Dannon to

[34] King, Julia. "Deep Thinkers." Computerworld, July 15, 2013, p. 24.

[35] Collett, Stacy. "Data Plus: Editor's Choice Awards 2013." Computerworld, August 26, 2013, p. 23.

[36] King, Julia. op. cit. p. 25.

target price cuts in areas where they will have the greatest effect, rather than incurring the business cost of across-the-board price cuts. [37]

- **Ford:** Ford Motor Co. is using big data analytics (including social media analytics) to drive business value in three specific areas: determining the features customers want (and don't want) in their cars, tailoring the bulk of production to those models and options that customers want most, and making sure dealerships have the right cars (with the right features) that customers in their geographical area want to buy.[38]

- **Daimler:** Daimler analyzes warranty and goodwill data along with vehicle ECU telematic data to provide early warning to Daimler engineers of potential part failures and quality issues, before large-scale service issues appear. They built their AQUA big data platform on Teradata's Active Enterprise Data Warehouse and the Microstrategy data visualization tool. The system can identify potential problems in vehicles that have only been on the road a few weeks, and can get them fixed before the customers experience vehicle failures.[39]

Note the common threads in all of these examples: the results of data analysis are delivered, in real or near-real time, directly to workers who can use the information most effectively and efficiently to improve business processes, manage customer and stakeholder relationships, and develop new products.

This is not your father's data warehouse!

---

[37] Waxer, Cindy. "Inside the Yogurt Wars." Computerworld, August 12, 2013: http://bit.ly/2axp1Bn.

[38] King, Julia. "Fueled by Analytics." Computerworld, December 2, 2013, pp. 13-18.

[39] Dullaghan, Anne. "Daimler Drives High Performance." Teradata Magazine, Q1 2011: http://bit.ly/2ae9ctQ.

Key Points

- "Perennial BI" is about a fundamental shift in thinking: from the static analysis of data at rest to the immediate consumption of data in motion, with appropriate responses.

- BI environments should be less like traditional gardens (where you just look at what's there) and more like outdoor living rooms (focused around activities).

- BI environments must support the movement, integration, consumption, and use of data in all forms, for all purposes, in all places, and at all times.

- "Perennial" (Agile) BI environments deliver the results of data analysis in real or near-real time, directly to workers who can use the information most effectively and efficiently to improve business processes, manage customer and stakeholder relationships, and develop new products.

- Perennial BI actively seeks out new sources of data that provide insights and challenge assumptions, enabling the enterprise to respond more quickly and effectively to changing business conditions.

- Perennial BI focuses on using information to empower front-line workers and improve operations, rather than on optimizing office decision-making.

Section IV
Weeds, Pests and Critters

As every experienced gardener knows, doing everything right is no guarantee of success. We've all experienced the frustration of placing an expensive plant in perfect soil, in a perfect location, with perfect nutrients, only to have it killed by weather, weeds, pests, or just plain bad luck!

Similar dangers exist in BI: metrics that don't tell us what we really need to know (or that tell us what we really don't want to know!), KPIs that drive unexpected (and unfortunate) behavior, incorrect interpretation of data, the substitution of "gut instinct" for data, unwarranted assumptions, and inappropriate application of analytics are all very real concerns. The consequences of these problems can range from minor annoyances to multi-million dollar losses that make the national news to—in one extreme case—the near collapse of the global economy!

In this section, let's take a look at some of the most common dangers—both technological and human—that threaten the success of every BI initiative.

Chapter 12
Weeds and Mulch

Every project—every human endeavor—is a minefield of risks and mitigations. You have to figure out how to either detonate the mines, detect the mines, or go around the mines to get to the other side.

Risks and mitigations are like weeds and mulch: the more time you spend mulching the soil, the less time you need to spend pulling weeds. But mulching the soil takes time away from planting seeds, so you need to be sure that your mitigation activities don't cause you to miss windows of opportunity (i.e. planting cycles). Remember, the purpose of a garden is to grow plants, not soil. But also remember that without good soil, you won't get good plants!

Let's take a quick look at some of the risks (weeds) associated with BI projects, and how we can best mitigate (mulch) them:

Risk 1: Failing to deliver BI results to the business in a timely manner. Some years ago, one of our divisions hired a consulting company to design and build a dealer data mart. They interviewed stakeholders, identified data sources and integrations, modeled the data, designed the schema, and more. After six months, they were ready to start creating the database and coding the ETL. Then, the business cancelled the project. Why? Because they'd been spending money for six months and hadn't seen any benefits! A few years later, that same division cancelled another BI project because the consultants told them it would take *one* month to deliver results! As business cycle times decrease, so does the business' patience with IT.

- **Mitigation 1**: Allow the business some "quick wins," via the "Quick Wins" and "Forklift" patterns described in Section 2. Make sure to deliver continuous value from your BI activities while you are working toward your target state BI architecture.

- **Mitigation 2**: Use Agile processes to reduce BI cycle times and eliminate inefficiencies in BI delivery. Strive for continuous improvement, and make sure the business sees the results of your work—and the continual improvement of your processes!

- **Mitigation 3**: Make sure that all BI projects are directed and governed by the business. Be transparent about obstacles that occur and partner with the business to come up with effective—and agreed upon—solutions.

Risk 2: Proliferation of BI tools, platforms and solutions. Once an organization gets "BI Religion", the result is often a proliferation of cults! Every department and division runs out and buys its own BI tools, platforms, databases, and solutions, from whatever vendor gets their ear first. This escalates IT support costs, and detracts greatly from the ROI on BI initiatives.

- **Mitigation 1**: Ensure that all BI work is done within the context of an overarching, enterprise-wide BI architecture. Reach a consensus across the business as to what BI capabilities are needed, and find (and fund) the minimal set of platforms and software needed to achieve them. Make sure you understand the long-range licensing and support requirements of any solution you purchase.

- **Mitigation 2**: Use POCs to identify the best solutions. For any given BI need, identify a small set of vendors with a good reputation for value delivery in this particular BI problem space. Work with the vendors to deliver a small, focused, time-boxed proof of concept[40] that solves a particular problem or delivers a defined piece of business value. Use the results of the POCs to evaluate and choose both the product that best meets your needs and the vendor you feel most comfortable partnering with.

- **Mitigation 3**: As you build toward your BI target state, work to consolidate solutions, platforms, and data. As data becomes more carefully defined and governed, move it into a central data repository and eliminate redundant data stores. As BI solutions coalesce around a more defined architecture, eliminate unneeded and redundant tools and platforms.

Risk 3: Insufficient IT or business resources. BI projects can demand a great deal of money and time for both IT (infrastructure and delivery) and the business (oversight and governance). During business cycles when resources are lean and funding is tight, how can BI be accomplished?

- **Mitigation 1**: To the greatest extent possible, build out BI capabilities and infrastructure as part of existing funded projects. For example, we are building out our operational data store (ODS) iteratively, in support of various Cloud applications we've purchased that require an integrated view of our Product, Customer, Service, Part, and Warranty data. At the same time, we are iteratively creating canonical data models around these business subject areas (which can be leveraged later in support of master

---

[40] This is similar to the agile concept of the "tracer bullet", a small and focused (but production quality) implementation of a larger and more complex user story. Like real tracer bullets, the objective is to help identify and focus on the target while in the act of shooting (i.e., delivering value to the customer). In other words: Ready, Fire, Aim!

data management), as well as canonical XML schema definitions for the web services that move data between the Cloud applications and the ODS.

- **Mitigation 2**: Fund and staff BI initiatives from the business divisions, not from IT. Business divisions are regarded as profit centers; IT is regarded as a cost center. Business divisions get funding and resources; IT does not. So, work with business divisions to identify business needs and problems that BI can address, help them identify the best vendors and products (again, within the context of your defined BI architecture), and work with them to obtain the necessary funding and staffing. Once you've helped the business take this step, do whatever is necessary to ensure the success of the project—once a BI project fails, you may not get a second chance!

- **Mitigation 3**: Evangelize BI across the organization, on the basis of risks, costs, and opportunity. In our company, for example, we emphasize the value of BI in ensuring regulatory compliance (a huge risk in our business), reducing costs associated with product failure and warranty replacement, and opening up opportunities for improved relationships with our customers and dealers. For example, using streaming data and predictive analytics to get products to dealers for servicing—before they break!

Risk 4: Multiple, uncertain, or inconsistent data meanings. We've already talked about the risk of delivering too little data (of high quality) too late; now we need to talk about the risk of delivering too much data (of low or uncertain quality) too soon! How do we mitigate the risk of giving the business the data it wants and needs if the data isn't right?

- **Mitigation 1**: Transparency, transparency, transparency! Remember, it isn't bad data per se that causes trouble; it's bad data that people don't know about. Use frequently updated and published metadata to keep the business informed about the data they're using: what it means, which business process creates it, which application manages it, which database it comes from, what computations or transformations alter it, how often it is updated, and how it's supposed to be used. Also, to the greatest extent possible, profile data values and proactively inform the business of values that appear to deviate from the norm.

- **Mitigation 2**: Let the business govern the data. Ultimately, it's the business that has to manage the trade-offs between risk (the risk of using data) and opportunity (the risk of *not* using data). Use metadata (as described above) to give the business the information it needs to manage these risks and make informed decisions about how and when to use the data for a particular business purpose. Provide the business with the infrastructure and tools needed to discuss and resolve questions and issues arising from data problems. Then use the results of data governance decisions by the business to improve both the data and the processes that create and manage them.

- **Mitigation 3**: Store data, not meaning. At the schema (storage) level, don't try to reconcile differing semantic perspectives and information needs. Unless you can quickly and easily get consensus on a common business definition of an attribute, don't try to shoehorn users into a single common meaning. Name, define, and store data based on its origin and use. If you need to create multiple occurrences of a data concept that has multiple meanings across the business, be sure to name and define these attributes in a way that makes the distinction in meaning clear. For example, if you can't arrive at a common business definition of *Last Activity Date*, create multiple attributes with names like *Last Warranty Claim Date*, *Last Product Service Date*, *Last Product Purchase Date*, and so on.

- **Mitigation 4**: Support multiple "views of the truth." Don't force all business users into a single representation of your company's data. Allow them the freedom to visualize the data they need in any form that delivers value to the business. This reduces the temptation for business users to demand that their particular data viewpoint be enforced at the data storage level. If a particular department wants to call *Last Product Service Date* "Last Activity Date," give that department a view that contains this name.

Risk 5: Being constrained by a non-extensible BI architecture. The BI product and platform landscape is constantly changing, and new BI capabilities are being created almost daily. You don't need all of these capabilities right now (some of them you may *never* need), but you need to be sure that your BI target state architecture is extensible enough to easily accommodate the new capabilities you decide your company needs.

- **Mitigation 1**: Focus your BI strategy around data, not technology. Always keep in mind that BI is about managing data assets for maximum value. Decide where and how it makes the most sense for your organization to enact this management.

- **Mitigation 2**: Focus on data in motion, not data at rest. BI strategies that center on data at rest (e.g. data warehouses and data marts) will be much less extensible than strategies focused on data in motion (e.g. streaming data and predictive analytics), even if these technologies are not immediately deployed in your organization.

Risk 6: Not enough (or too much) data governance. Not enough data governance invites BI process failure from bad or misunderstood data. Too much data governance strangles BI opportunity in IT red tape.

- **Mitigation 1**: Let the business (not IT) direct data governance efforts. Let the business decide how much governance they need, and how much risk they are willing to assume. IT should play a facilitation and support role, helping to broker the conversations and execute the decisions.

- **Mitigation 2**: Choose an approach that fits your company's culture. Top-down approaches to data governance only work in companies with a homogenous culture and a hierarchical organizational structure. More diverse companies may need to adopt the "non-invasive" approach of

Robert Seiner[41], or the "federated" approach of John Ladley.[42] Choose the approach that your business managers feel most comfortable with, or create your own approach if you need to.

- **Mitigation 3**: Start small, and focus data governance activities around the areas of greatest need. It's a mistake to try to manage everything all at once. Data governance processes are not "one size fits all", and not all data needs to be managed in the same way, or to the same degree. Data governance requirements should be determined and implemented iteratively, as data becomes better understood, and as uses for data are developed.

Risk 7: BI activities do not yield the anticipated results. The business is seeing fewer tangible benefits from BI and analytics than expected, and ROI is lacking.

- **Mitigation 1**: Ensure that all BI initiatives are directed at business activities. These include (but are not limited to) improving business processes, identifying new market or product opportunities, and managing stakeholder relationships.

- **Mitigation 2**: Ensure that all BI initiatives are associated with a measureable set of business metrics and KPIs (goals) that need to be met.

- **Mitigation 3**: Eliminate any human or organizational obstacles to becoming a data-driven company. This includes "gut thinking" decision-makers and departments mired in inefficient and manual processes. There is no practical difference between not knowing what to do and not doing what you know.

---

[41] Seiner, Robert S. *Non-Invasive Data Governance: The Path of Least Resistance and Greatest Success*. Technics Publications, 2014.

[42] Ladley, John. *Data Governance*. Elsevier/Morgan Kaufmann, 2012.

- **Mitigation 4**: Successfully manage the data you have before trying to get more. As Mitch Joel has said, companies that can't successfully manage "small data" have no chance of successfully managing "big data"!

- **Mitigation 5**: Fail as quickly and inexpensively as possible. Success is rarely assured on BI projects, and a certain amount of trial and error is almost always needed. Start with small, easily managed POCs until you know what works for you and what doesn't.

These are not, of course, all the risks that you will encounter on a BI project, nor all the mitigations available. But if you take a risk management approach to BI development, you are likely to be more successful than those who don't.

Key Points

- In all BI initiatives, allow the business to direct the management of risks and opportunities.

- Ensure that value is always being delivered to the business.

- Strive for continuous process improvement.

- Implement (or build toward) a single, consistent, enterprise-wide BI architecture.

- Ensure transparency of data, metadata and analytics across your organization.

- Focus your BI strategy on the application of data to business problems, not on BI technology.

Chapter 13
Mole Holes

It never fails: every spring and fall, I try to improve my backyard. Every spring and fall, a colony of moles turn my yard into a condominium development. It's not really their fault—they're just trying to find food and build nests. But while they're busy solving their own problems, they're creating problems for me. I've tried explaining this to them, but to no avail. At least twice a year, my beautifully manicured yard turns into the aftermath of the Battle of Dunkirk!

This happens in BI projects as well, and is one of the more common causes of BI project failure. Business users take the information that BI provides and use it to do things that are completely contrary to the best interests of their organization. They're not shooting *themselves* in the feet, you understand. From their point of view, they're using information to solve business problems. What they don't see are the "mole holes" (i.e. the unintended consequences) they are creating, into which other people (oftentimes, their company's customers and other stakeholders) are going to stumble and fall.

In BI, it's important to understand how the actions of human individuals can detract from the goal we're trying to reach. Human nature is often the shoal on which the ship of human endeavor is wrecked. Because BI is about the exchange of information among individuals and groups, BI success or failure is often determined by how individuals and groups use (or fail to use) information wisely.

We need to start by acknowledging a hard truth: while we humans like to think that we make rational decisions on the basis of fact, there is an increasing body of cognitive science that asserts otherwise. The truth seems to be that we make decisions intuitively and then rationalize them after the fact! So information is not so much the raw material of our decision-making; it's what tells us (after the fact) whether our decisions were correct. In a sense, information is like traffic signs; they don't so much direct our actions as they either confirm or contradict the assumptions we've already made about where we should be heading and how fast we should be driving. So it is important to understand the extent to which the application of analytics to data, and then to business problems, may be colored by inherent bias.

Data Bias

It is important to understand that humans do not always act on data in a logical or rational way; even when the data is good, the analysis of data itself may be skewed by human biases. With this in mind, the Data Science Association recently passed a Code of Professional Conduct[43] to address the following data analysis issues:

- *Cherry picking* data, while ignoring data that doesn't fit the analyst's preconceived view.

---

[43] Bertolucci, Jeff. "Data Scientists Create Code of Conduct." InformationWeek, October 7, 2013: http://ubm.io/2a03UXC.

- *Confirmation bias,* where variables that support the analyst's view are chosen over equally valid variables that do not.

- *Data selection bias,* where data sources that are most readily available (or favored by the analyst or his/her sponsor) are chosen over other possible sources of data.

- *Narrative fallacy,* where data is made to fit into a preconceived story line.

- *Cognitive bias,* where facts are skewed to fit beliefs rather than altering beliefs in the face of facts.

Without such a code of professional ethics, data analysts and data scientists can be unduly influenced by companies and organizations seeking to ratify their own agendas, regardless of the facts (as the Tobacco Institute did years ago, when they published "scientific" studies showing that nicotine was not addictive). To quote Michael Walker, President of the Data Science Association, "We educate people on these issues, and [data science] becomes a profession that follows a code of conduct. All of us can band together and tell an employer or client, 'No, we cannot do that. I'm not going to find evidence to support something you want to do, unless [the supporting data] is really there.'"[44]

MIS-APPLICATION OF ANALYSIS

Even when the results of data analysis are not skewed (either intentionally or unintentionally) by the analyst, they may still be applied inappropriately. Here are some real-life examples of the misapplication of analytics:

- Many insurance companies will raise the auto insurance premiums of people who take out home equity loans. Insurers say that there is a strong correlation between credit scores (which decrease when debt is

---

[44] Ibid.

taken on) and auto accidents. This is an example of equating correlation with causation. The fact that A seems to be associated with B does not mean that A causes B. It also begs the question of whether increased accidents are correlated with *all* debt, or just certain kinds of debt. Is someone who maxes out his credit card to play the slots at Vegas no more likely to have a car accident as someone who borrows to improve the value of his home?

- Insurance companies have also been accused of tracking people who buy plus-sized clothing online. This is an example of correlation without context. We don't know why people were making these purchases, or even who the purchases were for.

- Similarly, insurers have denied health-care coverage to people whose online purchases suggest even minor physical or mental health conditions.

- Some banks have been caught adjusting the credit scores of customers based on their social media associations. If your friends on Facebook or LinkedIn default on loans or have bad credit, you could be denied credit or forced to pay higher interest rates. The question to ask here is, "What stakeholder behavior is this policy intended to drive, and what is the desired business outcome?" The only behavioral outcome possible here is a lot of irate customers changing banks!

It's important to understand that the purpose of information (and hence, the purpose of BI) is to engage stakeholders in creative, value-producing ways. It is not to punish stakeholders for "inappropriate" behavior! Data (and information) is only as good as the relationships it supports.

These examples demonstrate a very important principle of analytics (or data science, if you will): there needs to be a grown-up in the room when the results of data analysis are applied to business problems and opportunities. It is essential that the results of data analytics are applied to business processes in ways that nurture and support both the organization's business goals and stakeholder relationships. Analytics that result in disaffected stakeholders, lawsuits, or public embarrassment clearly do not contribute business value to an enterprise![45]

MISUNDERSTANDING OF DATA

BI failures often occur when analysts or analytical processes use data they don't really understand or whose quality is uncertain. For example, analysts at one Fortune 1000 financial services company wanted to predict which call-center staff hires would stay on the job the longest. The results of the analysis showed that high-school dropouts were 2.6 times more likely to stay on the job than high-school graduates, and the analysts were ready to recommend that the company prioritize hiring of high-school dropouts for its call centers.[46]

An examination of the data, however, showed that different analysts had entered data from employee resumes in different ways, and had labeled the data differently, thus accounting for the error. One data entry person checked off all education levels that applied, while another checked only the highest level completed. Also, one analyst entered far more of the resumes related to employees who stayed longer than others did. These issues could have been avoided by making sure those performing data entry were assigned random groups of resumes to enter, and ensuring that input data was labeled consistently.

Other examples of this sort of error include CNN's reporting on Scotland's 2014 vote for independence from the United Kingdom: 58% Yes and 52% No. No one noticed that these figures added up to 110%. They were also incorrect in one other

---

[45] For more on this topic, please read Dr. Barry Devlin's excellent book *Business Unintelligence* (Technics Publications LLC, 2013).

[46] Mitchell, Robert L. "12 Predictive Analytics Screw-Ups." Computerworld, July 24 2013. http://bit.ly/2blsT7a.

important respect – Scotland had actually *rejected* independence by a vote of 45% Yes to 55% No![47]

This brings up another important principle of BI and analytics: a "smell test" should always be applied to the results! Knowledgeable people should be able to tell, based on prior experience or with reference to other company data or reports, whether a given set of results makes intuitive sense given the set of inputs. Don't accept the results of analyses without question; make sure they make sense for the business!

PROCESS IMPEDIMENTS

Human factors influence the outcome of BI initiatives in other ways as well:

- Refusing to change existing business structures or processes, even when the data suggests that taking a new or different approach will yield positive results. (The "we've always done it this way" argument.)

- Ignoring subject matter experts. (The sentiment of "I've been in this company 25 years! Who cares what a PhD just out of college thinks!")

- Trying to solve the wrong problem (e.g. building cheaper products instead of products of greater value).

- Sacrificing long-term vision to achieve short-term goals (e.g. making short-sighted spending cuts to temporarily increase stock value).

- Refusing to relinquish "turf" or ego for the greater good. One company's big data initiative went under because a senior developer was miffed at not having been brought onto the project earlier. Another project failed because a business owner refused to allow access to the data his business unit controlled.

---

[47] BBC. "Scottish referendum: Scotland votes 'No' to independence." September 19, 2014. http://bbc.in/1Dmu7Fw.

- The "Atlas Syndrome." Coined by Gartner VP Frank Buytendijk, this term describes IT people who try to do BI work independently of the business, believing that the business doesn't have the necessary technical understanding of the work involved. "As valid as this may seem, it results in a negative outcome."[48]

- Refusing to collaborate. On one failed BI project[49], the IT department ignored the business users' recommendation for a data analytics tool they wanted to use, and forced them to use a tool that didn't work for them or meet their needs (this tool cost less, and was more familiar to the IT people). The business people (who were the real subject matter experts) left and went to another company (one that used the tool they wanted). As Tricia Aanderud noted, IT's refusal to let the business use the tool it wanted destroyed their passion for and commitment to the entire BI initiative. So the business users took their passion elsewhere.

- Sabotaging of data. At one large financial institution, a marketing campaign sent letters to customers addressed to "Dear Idiot Customer John Doe." The inappropriate data had been entered into the customer service database by irate customer service representatives. In a similar case, journalist Lisa McIntire received a credit card offer from Bank of America addressed to "Lisa is a Slut McIntire." As with the "Dear Idiot" letters, the inappropriate data was probably entered into the credit card database by a disgruntled employee.[50]

Care must be taken to ensure that neither the results of data analysis nor their applications are skewed by logical fallacies, preconceived biases, organizational

---

[48] Gartner press release, February 24, 2005. http://gtnr.it/2ae94dW.

[49] Aanderud, Tricia. "3 Lessons Learned From One Dismal BI Failure" (blog posting). June 12, 2012. http://bit.ly/2af4IpX.

[50] Bedgood, Larisa. "Dirty Data Horror Stories – When Good Data Goes Bad" (blog posting, Dec. 8, 2014). http://bit.ly/2axp8Nj.

inertia, or intramural infighting. An organizational culture that rewards cooperation and teamwork will likely experience more success with BI initiatives.

DATA IS THE NEW WATER

As data and information become more pervasive and valuable within and across our organizations, we can expect to see more conflict over who controls the flow of data and information. We have seen this in the so-called "net neutrality" wars between Internet service providers and the federal government, and can expect to see increasing conflicts between data providers and the corporations that are increasingly dependent on them. I've seen this in my own company, which just switched providers of business information services.

Note that the problem lies not in the availability of data and information per se; it's in the availability of high-quality data and information that addresses specific business needs in a timely manner. For example, in many communities around the country, there is water of sufficient quality for agriculture, but not enough water suitable for drinking. Potable water must be brought in by truck, or purchased at a store. In the not-too-distant future, we will see attempts to "corner the market" on specific types of data and information needed by business and industry, restricting access and increasing the price. This will make it more difficult—or at least more expensive—for companies to get the data and information they need to survive.

"CITIZEN" DATA SCIENTISTS

The minefield of potential analytic pitfalls raises the issue of the so-called "Citizen Data Scientist": the business user or analyst who may not have any formal training in statistics but uses the new generation of data visualization and analytics tools to try to make sense of their data. How likely are they to run into the problems and issues described in this chapter?

First of all, I think it's important to understand that *anybody* can make the kinds of mistakes described in this chapter. Having a degree in Data Science doesn't guarantee success in BI and analytics, any more than having an MBA guarantees success in business. That being said, ignorance is always a greater predictor of failure than knowledge is. The more you understand the principles and concepts of statistics and data analysis, and the more you understand the tools you use and their limitations, the better your chances for success.

Dr. Fern Halper, in an excellent article in *Upside*[51], emphasizes the need for data analysts to get as much training in analytical methods and tools as possible. Don't just be a user of a data visualization tool; actually understand what the tool is doing (and not doing) with the data. Learn how to think about data, and about the process of turning data into actionable insight.

It is also important, as Halper notes, to have adequate controls in place to vet the results of data analyses before they are put to use. Or, as I put it earlier in this chapter, you must have a grown-up in the room before data is acted upon. Make sure to put "guard rails" on the process of turning data into information. This means vetting everything—the input data, the algorithms or models being employed, and the results of the analysis—before any use is made of the results.

Finally, it's essential to understand that all BI failures are, ultimately, human failures and not data failures. As I've always emphasized in my writings, a stakeholder approach is key to the success of any Agile endeavor—especially BI. Careful consideration must be given to the humans (and human processes) that create, manage, and use data and information. Data and information are only as good as the human relationships they support. Only to the extent that BI activities establish and maintain supportive, value-producing relationships among business stakeholders will those activities be successful. To do anything else will almost surely result in an embarrassing failure.

---

[51] Halper, Fern. "Two Tips for Citizen Data Scientists." *TDWI Upside*, 6/13/2016. http://bit.ly/2abZrCs.

Key Points

- Because BI is about the exchange of information among individuals and groups, BI success or failure is often determined by how individuals and groups use (or fail to use) information wisely.

- Humans do not always act on data in logical or rational ways; even when the data is good, the analysis of data itself may be skewed by human biases.

- Care must be taken to ensure that neither the results of data analysis nor their applications are skewed by logical fallacies, preconceived biases, organizational inertia, or intramural infighting.

- The purpose of information (and hence, the purpose of BI) is to engage stakeholders in creative, value-producing ways. It is not to punish stakeholders for "inappropriate" behavior!

- Data and information are only as good as the stakeholder relationships they support.

- An organizational culture that rewards cooperation and teamwork will likely experience more success with BI initiatives.

- Data is the new water, and we can expect to see increasing attempts to control access to it.

Chapter 14
Thugs and Slackers

There exist both a gardening and a data application of Gresham's Law: "Bad money drives out good money." In landscaping, we have the phenomenon that Ann Lovejoy refers to as "Thugs and Slackers."[52] These are plants chosen for convenience, without regard to their potential long-term impact on the landscape. "Thugs" may spread out of control, smothering and crowding out other plants in the garden. These plants must either be removed (if possible) or relegated to more "challenging" areas of the landscape where their "rampant energies" can be contained. At the same time, other carefully tended plants ("Slackers") may fail to thrive no matter how much they are nurtured; in these cases, the plants may benefit from being moved to a more suitable location, or—in extreme cases—removed entirely.

---

[52] Lovejoy, pp. 142-143.

In the data realm, we see a similar phenomenon: bad (or at least non-authoritative) data, grabbed quickly from the nearest available source by a business user with a deadline, travels (via Excel spreadsheets and Access databases) across business units with the speed of a virus, while data that is painstakingly collected, cleansed, transformed, and placed in a data warehouse or data mart may sit for years and never be used!

Students of economics will know that there is a corollary to Gresham's Law, called Thier's Law. It states that Gresham's Law holds true only if people believe (or are forced to accept) that there is no difference in intrinsic value between bad money and good money. If a shilling made of base metal is decreed, via legal tender laws, to have the same face value as a shilling made of pure silver, Gresham's Law observes that people will tend to hoard the silver coins and trade the less-valuable ones. But what if the legal tender laws are rescinded, and people are allowed to place their own value on coins? Given a choice, people would prefer to trade using the more valuable coin. In that case, Gresham's Law would work in reverse—good money would drive bad money out of circulation!

What this means for gardeners is that, given a choice of plants with which to solve a particular gardening problem, care must be taken to ensure that the correct choice is made. Plants must be chosen that will thrive in a given location without becoming invasive "thugs." What works well in one region (for example, ivy in France and kudzu in Asia) will be an invasive disaster in another region (for example, the U.S.). What works well in one location of the garden (e.g. along a fence line) will be hopelessly out of place in another (e.g. next to the house). All plants are not created equal, and choosing a plant for the garden because it is pretty or easily available may result in a large amount of work and expense that might have been avoided, had a more thoughtful choice been made.

What this means for data and BI architects is that while some initial business value may be achieved with suboptimal data, BI success over time depends on creating a store of high-quality data and encouraging its use. Business users must be able to discern good data from bad data, and to make good data choices. Remember that BI is, essentially, asset management of enterprise data assets; asset management involves not so much the management of the asset itself, but rather, the management of people's *behavior* toward the asset! For example, accountants don't really manage money; they manage how other people track and report their spending of money.

So, how do we create a "good currency" of high-quality, business-relevant, reusable data that can drive the "bad currency" of Excel and Access data out of circulation (or at least keep it under control)? We do this by introducing two very important BI processes: *data governance* and *master data management*.

Data governance can be defined as formal business oversight of rules and standards directing the management of data assets. Data management is the execution and implementation of these data rules and standards (usually by IT). Data governance by the business provides the direction for data management of enterprise data assets by IT.

Master data management (MDM) can be defined as the process of curating high-quality sets of data assets and disseminating them across the enterprise. The goal of MDM is not merely to create these "golden" sets of data about customers, products, retailers, etc., but to ensure that this data is used consistently across the organization—instead of other data that is less trustworthy or of lower quality.

These concepts lead us to an essential question: how can we promote the creation and use of "good currency" data in a manner consistent with the approach to BI that we have taken in this book—improving data assets gradually and iteratively while still delivering continuous business value from our BI infrastructure? To do this effectively, we fall back on Agile principles:

- Let the business direct the process, in response to recognized business needs.

- Maintain transparency of data assets across the organization, through the effective use of metadata. Make sure everyone has the information they need to make intelligent choices about where to find the data they need, and how to use it.

- Educate business users (continually!) on where and how to find good data, how to tell good data from bad data, how to determine when the results of analyses may be incomplete or incorrect, and how to report data errors and problems for resolution.

- Make sure that good data is quickly and easily available. Remember, Gresham's Law holds true only if people believe (or are told) that there is no difference between bad data and good data, or if getting good data is significantly harder than getting bad data.

- Focus data governance efforts less on data in isolation and more on data as it is actually used in the organization (i.e. when data problems result in BI process breakdowns, causing delays in creating accurate reports, metrics, analyses, or visualizations). Prioritize issues with bad data based on their actual costs to the organization, or the risks they present to critical business processes.

- Make use of business subject matter experts throughout the organization; these are the people best qualified to recognize data problems and suggest appropriate remediation. They are also usually the people most well-versed in using the data related to their area of the business.

- As better data is created, make sure it is published throughout the organization (e.g. pushed into application databases that need this data). Make sure that people know where and how to find this data, and how to use it. Also, make sure that less-trustworthy copies of this data are identified and deprecated.

- Don't try to boil the ocean—instead, create a workable process that can be executed iteratively to improve both the data and the data management/governance process over time.

There isn't time or space in this book for an exhaustive overview of data governance and master data management. The "Notes and Resources" section at the end of this book will point you to additional references on these topics. The important thing is to make sure your approach fits into the Agile framework of continuous engagement with the business, continuous (and incremental) value delivery, and continuous improvement.

Key Points

- As bad currency can drive good currency out of circulation, bad data can drive out good data under certain conditions: if people believe (or are told to accept) that there is no measureable difference between good data and bad data, or if good data is too hard to obtain compared to bad data.

- An Agile approach to data governance and master data management can gradually make good data more easily available and make bad data harder to obtain.

- These processes should be directed by the business, in response to business needs, and prioritized according to their importance to the business (as bad data either results in BI process failures or becomes a cost or risk to the business).

- Information about data (metadata) needs to be made available to business users, and they need to be educated on how to recognize bad data and respond appropriately.

- Data governance efforts should make effective use of the business subject matter experts already working in your business units.

Every gardener needs to develop a strategy for coping with a wide variety of garden pests, ranging from voracious insects (e.g. aphids and whiteflies) to snails and slugs, and from hungry critters (deer and rabbits) to destructive neighborhood dogs and cats. There are three possible approaches for dealing with pest problems:

1. Go nuclear and spread toxic chemicals (such as organo-phosphates) all around your garden. Try not to think about what this is doing to the environment and to the sustainability of your garden.

2. Fight nature with nature, counteracting destructive insects with beneficial ones (e.g. green lacewings and ladybugs), counteracting boring insects with beneficial nematodes (non-segmented roundworms) and using botanically-based insecticides and repellents (such as pyrethrins and bitrex).

3. Try to forestall potential pest problems through proper garden design. As strange as it may sound, most garden pest problems are caused by people, through practices such as planting shrubs right up against the sides of houses and decks, stressing plants with poor soil and poor drainage, and putting plants and shrubs in the wrong environments.

Pest problems exist in BI as well—these are bottlenecks and inefficiencies that are often the result of common but misguided approaches to BI development. Oftentimes, these bottlenecks are enough to throttle BI projects that become so bogged down in costly and time-consuming data definition, data cleansing, or data integration efforts that management is forced to pull the plug.

As suggested above, different approaches can be taken to solve these problems. Too heavy-handed an approach (for example, dictating designs or solutions by fiat) may create a toxic development environment that no one wants to participate in, or result in solutions that don't meet stakeholder needs. More Agile approaches will likely be more successful in finding creative solutions to problems that benefit all project stakeholders. And, of course, the best approach of all is to develop sustainable BI processes that keep these problems from occurring in the first place!

AGILE PRINCIPLES FOR BI BOTTLENECKS

So, what are some of the most costly and inefficient processes in BI development, and how do we eliminate or mitigate them?

The first one I can think of is the search for a common semantic meaning. In other words, an organization will provision no data until everybody in the organization agrees on some definition. Companies spend years, and millions of dollars, on this usually fruitless endeavor. And, of course, these meanings change constantly as the business changes (or else the static definitions keep the business from changing), so the value of this effort is problematic.

How do we eliminate this pest? Through a combination of data abstraction, data transparency and data governance. Instead of trying to constrict your entire business with a single set of definitions, use views and other forms of data virtualization to give each area of the business the representation of the data that it needs. Document these differing representations using metadata and share them with the business.

Use these differences as an opportunity to have a conversation about data governance (that is, a conversation among data stakeholders as to whether this is the same data or different data, what it should be called, and how it should be used). Then, as agreements are reached, implement changes into your enterprise data repository and associated information views, and update the associated metadata. Repeat this process as needed.

I realize that the idea of abandoning a common business definition of "data" is not going to sit well with my fellow data management professionals. I'm not saying that a common definition is an impossible outcome. All I'm saying is that you shouldn't let the search for common business meanings impede the delivery of data (and value) to the business. There are four key Agile principles at work here:

- *Focus on delivering business value as early and continuously as possible.*

- *Ensure transparency of all data, actions, and decisions.*

- *Empower business users to solve their own problems.*

- *Defer work to the point where the work actually needs to be done.*

In other words, address the problem at the point where it actually becomes a problem. Use metadata to provide transparency to the problem of differing business data definitions. Give the business a data governance structure and process that enables them to have the necessary stakeholder conversations and decide on a solution. Iteratively drive the organization toward better data meanings and higher-quality data, while still getting as much value as you can from the data meanings that currently exist.

A second problem involves implementing data meanings into the schema of the database. This mistake is often made in data warehouses and dimensional data marts. If the meaning of the data is incorporated into the structure of the database, then you'll end up refactoring the database schema every time the meaning of the data changes, or as business information requirements change, or as new requirements arise. If you find yourself continually refactoring your BI data stores in response to new information requirements from the business, you should recognize this as a red flag, and make use of one of the principles from my earlier book:

- *Always try to refactor at the highest possible level of abstraction.*

In other words, store data in as content-neutral a form as possible, and implement semantic meanings and business information requirements as much as possible at some higher level of abstraction (e.g. in a database view or some other form of data virtualization). In this way, as meanings change and new requirements arise, the information view layer can be quickly and easily changed without the effort and risk associated with refactoring the database schema.

A third problem area involves the movement of data into the data repository (usually referred to as ETL - Extract, Transform and Load, or ELT - Extract, Load and Transform). Horrendous amounts of time and effort are spent coding, testing, and maintaining the processes that move data into and out of our data stores. This is a classic example of an unsustainable process, and brings out another Agile principle:

- *Where possible, either eliminate or automate inefficient processes.*

Depending on your BI target state goal, eliminating ETL/ELT may or may not be possible. One option to consider is the use of a data virtualization portal to create what is sometimes called a "virtual data warehouse"; this approach makes data easily available without having to move it out of the source systems. Another approach was described earlier in the "Forklift" Pattern; this still requires the movement of data but requires much less cleansing and transformation than the traditional data warehouse approach.

If an ETL or ELT process is needed, the next best approach is to automate this process. There are tools available (some vendors that come to mind are Wherescape, Birst, Attunity, and Informatica) that provide model-based environments for ETL/ELT design. Using the designer, you model the process, deploy it, and schedule it for execution. There is no coding, and nothing but the model to maintain. This is a much more sustainable solution to the ETL/ELT problem than, for example, creating numerous SSIS (SQL Server Integration Services) packages that must be debugged, deployed, and maintained.

A fourth area of concern involves tasks such as data modeling, data mapping, and the collection of metadata. On BI projects, much time and effort is spent in these areas; a lot of this work becomes little more than documentation, usually out of date and of little or no value. This is not to say that these things can't or shouldn't be done; they just need to be done thoughtfully. The Agile principles here are:

- *Make sure the right work is done at the right time, by the right people, in the right way, and for the right reasons.*

- *Working products are preferable to comprehensive documentation.*

- *The team owns the work (and all artifacts associated with the work).*

- *Strive for simplicity (defined as "the art of maximizing work not done").*

- *Agile approaches must lead to sustainable development; that is, the development of solutions should not require undue exertion, nor impose an onerous support burden on any project stakeholder.*

In *Building the Agile Database*, I described an Agile approach to data modeling in terms of model-driven development (MDD): the data model is jointly owned, and used to bring stakeholders together to achieve a common understanding of a problem to be solved and of the solution to that problem. Then, the model is used to generate or build part of the solution (for example, a database schema or object class, or the schema definition of a web service). At each iteration of the model, collaboration between stakeholders is taking place, knowledge and understanding are being increased, and value to the customer is being created. This is the difference between an Agile model and "big design up front" (BDUF), which makes Agile developers cringe!

Another example is the infamous data dictionary: a common artifact of BI projects which documents data sources, characteristics (such as data type, length, and nullability), transformations, computations, and more. This data is usually maintained laboriously in something like a spreadsheet, and is usually out of date the moment it's created. Keeping the data dictionary current and usable becomes almost a full-time job on some BI projects!

There are numerous ways of solving this problem. For example, many vendors sell tools that make it easier to create, manage, and publish metadata (and keep it current!). The basic questions to ask before choosing a solution approach are: Who needs to have what information about the data? When? Why? In what form does this information need to be provided? Whose responsibility should it be to capture this data, publish it, and keep it current?

Here's one low-budget approach I've used on past projects: as the data modeler, I'm involved in all the stakeholder discussions around data requirements (including the selection of data sources, identification of integrations and transformations needed, etc.). So it makes a certain amount of sense for me to "scribe" (that is, to capture) the results of these discussions in the data model—provided that this information can be kept current (which is not a problem if I'm included in all the data discussions) and can be published quickly and easily in a consumable form to the stakeholders who need the information.

This approach involves the creation of user-defined properties (UDPs) in the data model. UDPs are metadata fields that can be used to capture supplemental information about the data (e.g. the source of the data or the application/system that maintains it). Since my data modeling tool allows me to create UDPs at any level of the model, I've created several UDPs in the model template that I use as the starting point for any new data model. For example, I define Source System and Source Table at the entity level, and Source Column and

Transformation/Computation at the attribute level. I capture assumptions and agreements concerning data requirements, along with same data values, in Notes objects in the model, tagged with keywords such as "Assumption:", "Agreement:", "Change:", "User Story:", "Sample Data:", and so on.

I can then extract and report any of this data by querying my modeling tool's metadata repository. The tool gives me the ability to create PDF reports in any format I wish, and spreadsheet (CSV) extracts as well. I generate a set of standard reports which are usually posted to a project SharePoint site, along with PDFs of the logical and physical data models. Since the data is captured during the process of discussing the data requirements, and can be published quickly and easily, creating and maintaining a data dictionary is no longer a time-consuming and arduous process that often excludes key stakeholders and delivers little value.

The reason it's so important to identify and remove these bottlenecks is to ensure support for the following two Agile principles:

- *Welcome changing requirements, even late in development; Agile processes harness change for the customer's competitive advantage.*

- *It's more important to respond to change than to follow a plan.*

In one BI project I worked on, the business analyst laboriously created a large set of data interface documents and specifications describing the source-to-target data mapping. When I requested a change to one of the data attributes, I was told that nothing could be changed because it would require updating all the documentation. This is how you know that you don't have an Agile process—if your project documentation prevents you from being able to make changes, your project isn't Agile!

I mentioned standards and governance earlier in this chapter, and that subject deserves some discussion now. On the surface, standards (e.g. data modeling standards, ETL development standards, and application coding standards) and governance (e.g. code reviews and quality testing) might seem to impede, rather than promote, agility. So let's introduce some further Agile principles to put this in perspective:

- *Catch mistakes as early as possible, to minimize the effort and expense of refactoring.*

- *Avoid reinventing the wheel—doing what someone else has already done isn't Agile!*

It's important to recognize that there's a trade-off here: delivering an incomplete solution to business users can still deliver value, but delivering a defective or unusable solution may get your project cancelled. It's important to ensure that what you deliver meets your customers' expectations of quality.

You also want to ensure that team members aren't wasting time answering the same questions and solving the same problems over and over again. Well-written (and not excessively detailed) standards can provide much-needed guidance to developers, speed the development process, and result in a higher-quality product that is easier to support and maintain.

We have, for example, documented standards for data model development (e.g., an attribute name must end with a classword that describes its domain, such as Identifier, Quantity, Description, Name, or Date). This ensures that anyone working with this data, such as an application developer or business user, knows at a glance what sort of data values to expect.

Standards for developers are similar to metadata for end users, and are created for much the same reason: to answer questions, reduce uncertainty about what to do, prevent the wasting of time and effort, and reduce the amount of rework required to correct easily preventable mistakes.

Lastly, let me mention one of the most important principles of Agile:

- *Strive for continuous improvement; each iteration of a project should deliver more value more easily, and at lower cost.*

For example, I've learned to leverage many of the capabilities of my data modeling tool to help me deliver better results in much less time. I use macros and option sets to generate a database DDL from my models for any target database platform, with no manual tweaking required; the DDL can be run directly in the database to create the necessary data structures, keys, indexes, and constraints.

I use logical-to-physical name mapping to instantly convert entity and attribute names in the logical model to table and column names (abbreviated if necessary) in the physical model. For example, the attribute name *Consolidated Bill-To Address* in the logical model can appear as CONS_BILL_TO_ADDR in the physical model.

In addition to the standard metadata reports described previously, I've also created reports that alert me to quality defects in the data model. For example, I have reports that identify entities and attributes with no business definitions, entities with no identified data sources, and attributes with no domain assignments. This helps ensure that the models are complete and correct before they are published!

Depending on the BI approach your organization is taking and the amount of money they're willing to spend, both the problems and the solutions may be different from those described above. The important takeaway here is to learn to recognize inefficiencies and bottlenecks in your BI development process, then use Agile principles to correct them.

Key Points

- Examples of BI processes that can require too much time, cost, or effort include: semantic definition of data, data modeling, creation of a "data dictionary" or other metadata, creation and maintenance of ETL/ELT processes, and refactoring of database schemas.

- Use the following Agile principles to help you identify and eliminate bottlenecks and obstacles to your BI development:

  o Focus on delivering business value as early and continuously as possible.

  o Ensure transparency of all data, actions, and decisions.

  o Empower business users to solve their own problems.

  o Defer work to the point where the work actually needs to be done.

  o Always try to refactor at the highest possible level of abstraction.

  o Where possible, either eliminate or automate inefficient processes.

  o Make sure the right work is done at the right time, by the right people, in the right way, and for the right reasons.

  o Working products are preferable to comprehensive documentation.

  o The team owns the work (and all artifacts associated with the work).

  o Strive for simplicity (defined as "the art of maximizing work not done").

  o Agile approaches must lead to *sustainable development.*

  o Welcome changing requirements, even late in development.

  o It's more important to respond to change than to follow a plan.

  o Catch mistakes as early as possible.

  o Avoid reinventing the wheel.

  o Strive for continuous improvement.

- Learn to recognize inefficiencies and bottlenecks in your BI development process, then use Agile principles to correct them.

Section V
The Sustainable Garden

In this final section of the book, I'd like to focus on maintaining and supporting your BI environment. Prior to its recent resurgence, BI had fallen out of favor at many companies, primarily because the time and expense of upkeep of a BI environment has been so prohibitively expensive.

One of the principal maxims of data management is that the cost of creating, maintaining, and disposing of data should not exceed the value it returns to the enterprise. This also needs to be true of BI: the cost of creating and maintaining your BI infrastructure should never exceed the value that your organization derives from it!

As we've already noted, a sustainable garden is one which requires less effort, cost, and upkeep with each passing year. We need to set a similar goal for our BI environment. So let's take a look at the things that make both gardens and BI infrastructure hard to take care of!

Chapter 16
Sustainable BI

What do you think of when you hear the word "garden"? Many people think of formal English gardens, with their neat rows of carefully arranged and artfully managed blooms. What we tend to forget is that those English country estates employ dozens of workers and spend vast amounts of money.

A garden can be many things. It can be, in Ann Lovejoy's words, a "toxic monster" that devours time, money, and energy, and harms the environment with toxic chemicals. Or it can be a "green haven" that shelters both humans and wildlife, is easy to sustain, and conserves natural resources. Most of us have had experiences with the first type of garden: the garden that requires constant weekends of weeding, mulching, and pruning. Very few of us have experienced the joy of a sustainable garden—one which actually requires *less* work with each passing year.

What is the difference that makes a sustainable garden? (Or, to get back to this book's actual topic, a sustainable BI architecture?) I think it's a combination of foresight, process, and attitude. As Ann Lovejoy puts it, "the essence of garden design is either cooperation or control."[53] A control-based approach tries to force nature into an unnatural form and hold it there; the design of the garden doesn't correspond to how people actually interact with nature (or nature with people). Sustaining this unnatural design takes more work than a natural design would require, and delivers less value (satisfaction) to the end user. What made English gardens possible was the fact that the people creating the gardens didn't have to do the work of maintaining them!

An unsustainable approach to BI is very much like an English garden: its design doesn't support the way that people naturally interact with data, and the structures created require constant maintenance and support. Moreover, these structures hold data in a rigid and non-extensible form, and are difficult to change quickly in response to changing business information needs. Ask yourself this question: if your BI staffing was suddenly reduced by half[54], what would happen to your BI infrastructure? Would it begin to crumble and collapse? Would you be unable to support your customers? Then you don't have a sustainable BI architecture!

Let's look at some of the characteristics of a sustainable garden and BI infrastructure.

SUSTAINABLE BI ARCHITECTURE

The essence of architecture is *fitness for purpose:* understanding how people will interact with the end product. This is why the architect who designs your house

---

[53] Ibid, page 133.

[54] This is analogous to what happened in England after the World Wars, when increases in labor costs made it impossible to employ the number of people necessary to maintain English estates.

will first ask all sorts of questions about your lifestyle, family, entertainment habits, and more. The design of a house (or anything else) needs to support the way people will use it.

In gardening, as I mentioned earlier, the key question is: "How do you want to be in the garden, and what do you want the garden to do for you?" In BI, the key question is: "How do people naturally want to interact with data, and what do they want data to do for them?" All design is governed by an overarching architectural viewpoint; this viewpoint, in turn, is governed by these key questions of usage.

Think, for example, about how our business customers interact with data in the BI environments we typically create for them. First, they have to submit a request to IT, then give us requirements, which are formally documented. The request usually necessitates the creation or modification of data structures in a data warehouse or data mart, as well as the creation or modification of one or more ETL packages. Data has to be identified, sourced, mapped, profiled, cleansed and transformed. Access permissions to the database must be set up. And then the business user *still* needs to map, cleanse, and transform data in their visualization tool, to put it in a form suitable to that user's information need! Is it any wonder that IT organizations often spend millions of dollars creating BI solutions that nobody ever uses?

What this tells us is that a well-architected BI solution removes IT as the bottleneck between users and their data, and allows them to access their data whenever and however they like. It also tells us that the semantic and informational characteristics of data need to be defined by the business, not by IT. One of the reasons that IT-created BI solutions often go unused by the business is that the IT-sanctioned view of the data embodied by data warehouses and data marts doesn't correspond to the business users' view of the world, and often excludes meaningful data that doesn't fit the preapproved database schema.

Apart from ensuring that the end product actually suits the intended use and delivers the intended value, architecture helps create solutions that are both *reusable* and *extensible:* solutions that are applicable to more than one problem and that can be easily modified to accommodate future needs. Again, think about what usually happens in our IT-created BI environments when business data definitions or business information needs change. This usually requires a painful and time-consuming redesign of the database schema, along with modifications to ETL packages. What this should tell us is that our data needs to be stored in a way that doesn't require painful redesign of database structures when data needs to be added or changed.

Moreover, extending or modifying data structures must be accommodated in a way that doesn't impact users of the solution. It should be apparent that the storage of data must be kept separate from any semantic or informational meaning ascribed to it, so that data structures don't need to be modified when business meanings or information needs change (as they will, constantly, over time).

In addition, a well-architected solution is *sustainable*, delivering increasing value at decreasing cost over time. Almost any BI solution is going to require some up-front cost and effort to implement data platforms, design databases, and provision data. However, this effort should diminish over time, as existing data becomes increasingly reused and tools and processes are put in place to make accommodating future requests easier. If the BI solution you put in place, say, five years ago still requires the same (or greater) cost and effort to support, you've done something wrong.

SUSTAINABLE BI DESIGN

The design of the solution needs to support an incremental progression of work that leads ultimately to the end goal (or "target state") of the architecture while providing value at each step. Moreover, it should do so in a way that makes the final product easy to support and sustain. In gardening, for example, we replace rectangles and straight lines in our landscape designs with smoothly-flowing curves; this eliminates hard-to-mow corners and simplifies edging. We replace narrow rows of plants with mounded clusters of plants; this creates a more natural landscape and reduces weeding. We try to reduce or eliminate lawns, which require lots of work to maintain. Design considerations for a BI solution should follow naturally from the sustainability requirements of the target state architecture, namely:

- Data should be made quickly and easily available to any authorized user, with an absolute minimum of IT intervention.

- Business users should be able to navigate through and obtain meaning from data in a natural and intuitive way.

- Data should be stored in a content-neutral state (i.e. as data, not as information), in a structure that is quickly and easily modifiable and extensible.

- Data meaning should be defined by the business, and implemented in a form that is separate from the storage of the data and easily modified as business meanings and information needs change.

- The process of provisioning data needs to be as streamlined as possible, making use of tools and processes that minimize the amount of effort required.

- Data governance structures and processes need to be non-invasive, and must work in parallel with data and information delivery processes. They must not impede getting needed data to the business.

SUSTAINABLE BI IMPLEMENTATION

The way a garden design is implemented determines the amount of work required to sustain it. Using native plants, for instance, creates a more sustainable garden that requires less watering and fertilizing. Mulching and composting is less work than weeding and raking, and ensures adequate nutrition for plants. Choosing shrubs that are the right size for your landscape eliminates the need for constant pruning.

Perhaps the most challenging aspect of a BI project is deciding how much of the effort needs to be front-loaded and how much can wait until later. You want to avoid approaches that require too much "wait" time. As a general rule, if you can't start delivering results within a month, your BI project will probably fail.

At the same time, you also want to avoid approaches that will later require large amounts of "scrap and rework" processes. There's always a trade-off between work that you should do now, in order to avoid more work later, and work that can be done incrementally as your project develops.

In landscaping, for example, some hardscape work (setting paths, putting in wiring for lights) should be done up-front so as to save excess work and disruption to the garden later. Other work, such as setting herbaceous borders, can be done at almost any time.

Some sorts of BI work will repay some initial investment of effort; for example, making sure that data is always acquired from its most authoritative source. Other BI-related tasks, such as ETL development, cry out for as much automation as you can afford, as they are major bottleneck points in any BI project. Always be cognizant of the value that is generated from any piece of work; direct efforts toward the most value-producing work and try to automate or eliminate tasks that require substantial effort and return minimal value.

The BI pattern progression we examined previously describes an approach to the implementation of the BI architecture and design requirements mentioned above. In these BI patterns, we're trying to do a number of different things all at once. We're trying to let our business customers determine how they want to interact with data; at the same time, we are trying to learn from our customers' experiences to inform our BI development process. We're trying to create a BI infrastructure that supports the ways in which our customers need to get value from data, and then progress incrementally toward that target state, while delivering value at each intermediate step. We're also trying to create a sustainable BI infrastructure: one which doesn't require an untenable amount of staffing and support to remain viable, and one which is easily modifiable and extensible as new technology becomes available and business information needs change.

A major emphasis of the Agile approach is making sure that the right work (and *only* the right work) is done at the right time, and in the right way. You should always keep the end goal in mind when deciding what needs to be done when.

SUSTAINABLE BI PROCESS

It's important to understand that the process of reaching the end goal involves a series of smaller intermediate steps. It's also important to realize that the end goal needs to be kept in mind at each step; otherwise, you risk going off-course and wasting time and resources. The pattern progression described earlier is an example of what Ann Lovejoy calls "working toward," where each step in the process is informed by an awareness of the end goal or target state. At each point, we ask ourselves, "How will this step move us forward to our eventual goal?" This helps us avoid wasted effort or, worse, work that diverts us down a side path, away from our goal.

Each intermediate step should create immediate value for the customer while moving the project closer to the target state. It's also important to understand that the conclusion of each intermediate step will trigger a reassessment of both the process ("What could we have done better?") and the end goal itself ("Is this really where we want to be going?").

Improving the process will help us achieve our goal more quickly, but the process of creating our BI infrastructure may change our initial vision of the target state. As with landscaping, the final product may not be what you originally envisioned, but if you keep the key requirements in mind at each step, you will eventually get to where you need to be.

The process of developing a BI infrastructure involves almost constant decision-making. What tasks need to be done now; which can be deferred until later? Which tasks have higher priority? Which tasks return the greatest amount of business value? Which tasks must be done sequentially, and which can be done concurrently? Here is where an Agile methodology can be of great help, since the concept of Agility enables projects to manage work in a way that maximizes opportunity and minimizes risk.

Since Agile methods aim to maximize the value created for a given amount of work, there are two very important concepts to keep in mind on an Agile project: *reusability* and *automation*. At every step, ask whether there are existing patterns or solutions that can be reused to save the time and effort of reinventing the wheel. Also ask whether tools exist (or can be quickly made or bought) to automate time-intensive or labor-intensive work.

An Agile approach also involves continual questioning of the work we are doing. Is this work really necessary? Can it be done differently, with better tools or in a more cost-effective manner? The hallmark of an Agile approach is continual improvement. Consider, for example, the following passage from Ann Lovejoy's book:

> "I learned how to make gardens sustainable by questioning every established design principle I knew, asking myself if the old rules and techniques really made sense today. Do I really need to double or triple dig each bed? (No. Layering amendments works fine and is far less work.) Must I divide and reset the perennial beds every three years or so? (Yes, so I no longer make traditional perennial beds.)"[55]

Another hallmark of the Agile process is a willingness to experiment (within reasonable limits) with new tools and techniques. Ann Lovejoy continues her journey of sustainability with the following words of wisdom:

> "I needed to reevaluate everything I knew about garden design and maintenance. I like experimenting, so I began making many kinds of beds, applying ideas I had learned about sustainable agriculture and organic farming to the garden. Over time, I developed a method of bed making that has proved both attractive and long-lastingly effective…The resulting system pleases me very much, especially because it is so flexible that it can be adapted to suit any style of garden you might want."

---

[55] Ibid, page 5.

In summary, any truly Agile approach will have the following hallmarks:

- *Cooperative* – includes all stakeholders in the process.
- *Dynamic* – continually improving in response to changing needs and new technologies.
- *Exploratory* – looks for new ways of delivering value.
- *Flexible* – open to new ways of doing things.
- *Reusable* – can be leveraged to solve future problems.
- *Sustainable* – delivers continual value over time with less effort.

The time spent in planning, designing, and creating a sustainable BI solution will be repaid many times over in reduced support costs, faster responsiveness to customer needs, and greatly increased customer satisfaction (not to mention more willing customer support for future BI initiatives!).

SUSTAINABLE BI GOVERNANCE

To ensure the maximum quality of data and information, and its maximum value and usability across the organization, some degree of governance is both reasonable and inevitable. However, it's important to implement governance in a way that doesn't unreasonably forestall the benefits that data and information—even imperfect data and information—can provide.

Data governance and information governance can best be thought of as twin guard rails on each side of the BI highway. Data governance, on the one hand, serves to identify and correct problems with data quality, currency, and consistency as they arise. This helps ensure the best possible value from the use of data assets at the least risk.

Information governance, on the other hand, helps identify issues with the output of data analyses and visualizations. Information governance helps ensure both the appropriateness and reusability of information created from data, so that its application to business needs promotes, rather than discourages, the stakeholder interests of the enterprise.

In all cases, governance processes should be driven by the business in response to business needs, and should emphasize the gradual and iterative improvement of an organization's data and information capabilities over time. In no respect should governance be an impediment or roadblock to the process of delivering value to the business from the timely and correct use of data and information. Again, the goal of governance is not to ensure perfection; it's to ensure the greatest value at the least risk.

Key Points

- An unsustainable approach to BI is very much like an English garden: its design doesn't support the way that people naturally interact with data, and the structures it creates require constant maintenance and support.

- A sustainable BI environment maximizes flexibility of data use and minimizes control of data and data structures.

- A sustainable BI environment requires a sustainable *architecture*, *design*, *implementation,* and *process*.

- A sustainable BI environment also requires a sustainable BI governance process that acts as a "guard rail" to data and information use without becoming a roadblock.

- Key concepts in sustainable BI are: *fitness for purpose, extensibility, flexibility, reusability, automation of processes,* and *continuous improvement*.

- A truly Agile approach to BI is *cooperative, dynamic, exploratory, flexible, reusable,* and *sustainable*.

There is never any one factor that guarantees success—in gardening or in anything else in life. But there are any number of things that will ensure failure. Most gardeners are familiar with what might be called "critical success factors" in gardening: soil amendment, frequent mulching with compost, adequate watering, to name a few. Similarly, there are "critical success factors" for landscapers: ensure that the landscape takes into account the needs of the customer and how the customer wants to interact with the landscape, for instance.

Similarly, success in BI depends on our awareness of the critical success factors that often determine the outcomes of BI initiatives. To sum up some of the major points of this section (and a few that haven't previously been made), here is a list (not necessarily exhaustive) of critical success factors for the successful implementation of any BI solution:

1. The impact of the BI solution on the organization's IT infrastructure (network, servers, storage) is fully understood and provisioned.
2. Staffing and administration requirements for the solution are fully understood and provisioned.

3. Licensing and support costs are fully understood and funded, and increases in costs over time are known and provided for.

4. Data storage requirements, and expected growth of data over time, are fully understood and provided for. This includes storage for the output of analyses.

5. The BI solution supports a well-defined and well-governed process for business intelligence and analytics. This process, in turn, supports and reinforces the organization's data management, data governance, process improvement, and stakeholder management processes.

6. The data structures and information views that support BI queries, reporting, and analyses are well-designed and usable by the business.

7. Security requirements for both the source (repository) data and the BI output are well-understood and enforced.

8. Data analyses are well-defined and focused, addressing specific business needs and pain points.

9. Data analyses support an iterative process of continual improvement within the organization.

10. Business users are willing to be "data-driven," basing their business decisions on the evidence of data, rather than on "gut instinct" or past history.

11. Business expectations regarding the quality and currency of data are well-informed and realistic.

12. Business expectations of the business value of BI technology are realistic. There are no "silver bullets" for the business.

13. Business decisions based on analytical data are made for the purpose of engaging customers and other business stakeholders in creative and mutually profitable ways, and encourage positive behavioral changes.

14. Data (both input and output) is well-managed, ensuring that input data is both current and high-quality, and that output data is not kept past its useful life. The cost of managing this data does not exceed its value to the company.

15. Data (both input and output) is properly documented in a metadata repository that is accessible to all users. This repository also contains company-wide standard KPIs and data definitions.

16. The results of data analyses are both repeatable (that is, they can be rerun with fresh data at any time) and reusable (that is, users in other departments and divisions—if authorized—can make use of analysis without having to "reinvent the wheel").

17. Different levels of IT support exist to ensure that advanced business users can do their work with a minimum of interference, while less-experienced users can get whatever support and assistance they need.

18. A mature data governance process either exists in the organization (and is being reinforced by the BI solution), or the BI solution is being used to support the creation of such a process.

19. Master data repositories either exist in the organization (and are used and updated by the BI solution), or the BI solution is being used to support the creation of such repositories.

20. A sufficient amount of training is given to business users, administrators, and IT support staff to enable the efficient and effective use of the solution.

21. Data updates are applied in appropriate ways, at appropriate levels of the solution stack. For example, updates to an ODS should always be done in a controlled manner, either through batch updates or via web services. No ad-hoc updating of the ODS (or any BI data source) should be permitted.

22. The inherent risks involved in data discovery and analytics are well-understood and well-managed.

23. Users are able to combine data from the repository with local data (e.g. spreadsheets) and data from other sources to create data "mashups" and other visualizations.

24. Business intelligence competency centers (BICCs) are established both in IT and in business units throughout the company.

25. The top-level executive is continually available to help promote and direct BI efforts.

Success in a BI initiative is also predicated on an organization's ability to successfully manage "small data." Mitch Joel, among others, has noted that unless an organization is actively working to get its data out of application databases and transformed into "actionable insights," then it probably will not benefit from any BI initiative.[56]

Key Points

- There are critical success factors (things that must be done) associated with any endeavor, as well as critical risks that must be avoided. In order to ensure the best odds of success, we must be aware of those things we must do, and those things we must avoid doing.

- One very important critical success factor is that the BI solution supports a well-defined and well-governed process for business intelligence and analytics. Nothing that does not support a business process will further a business objective, or provide measureable business value.

- The business must always be completely involved with, and supportive of, the BI process. They must be fully aware of the quality of the data they are working with, they must be fully trained in the use of their tools, and they must be capable of making use of the results of analyses in a sensible and constructive way.

- BI activities should always result in an improvement of business processes and/or a strengthening of relationships with business stakeholders. They should address specific business needs and pain points, and should support continuous improvement of business capabilities.

- BI processes should support (and be supported by) a mature, organization-wide data and information governance process that ensures both high-quality data and reusable, business-relevant information.

- Top-level executive support for BI initiatives is critical to BI success.

- Companies should work to improve their "small data" capabilities and processes before taking on larger-scale BI initiatives such as "big data," real-time predictive analytics, and Complex Event Processing.

---

[56] Joel, Mitch. "The Problem With Big Data (It's Not Me, It's You)." Blog post, July 3, 2013: http://bit.ly/2axpWS1.

Section VI
Case Study

To illustrate the application of the concepts in this book, I'm going to continue the saga of a fictional company called "Blue Moon Guitar Company"[57]. The company designs and builds custom guitars and other wooden stringed instruments to order. When ordering an instrument, the customer can specify a number of customization options, such as size, finish, type of wood used, and more. Each model of instrument is associated with a set of these customization options, and each option specified contributes to the total list price of the instrument.

The company has different manufacturing divisions, each of which makes instruments under a particular brand name. The divisions are more or less autonomous, and are allowed to set their own prices. Each division has its own factories, and costs of parts (components of each instrument) and labor (for assembly) vary by location for each factory. Part and labor cost data for each factory is maintained in databases on the company's central mainframe computer.

---

[57] I created this fictional company as the Case Study in my first book, *Building the Agile Database*.

Pricing Managers at each division input and manage the customization options for each model of instrument made by that division. Each option/model combination can be associated with an assembly of parts (either individual parts or part structures) called a *configuration*. The aggregate of parts and labor data for each configuration is factored into a set of calculations that determines the base price of the instrument before any discounting is applied. Option, option/model, configuration, and pricing data is kept separate by division, and the data for a division can only be viewed and updated by that division's Pricing Managers.

Each model of instrument has a standard configuration, consisting of a set of standard options. Each standard option is associated with a standard assembly of parts; these assemblies can be shared by more than one standard option. Options are added to or removed from the standard configuration to create a custom instrument.

Blue Moon also has a subsidiary division that sells aftermarket replacement parts to customers and guitar shops around the world.

IDENTIFYING THE DATA

Blue Moon occupies a specialty niche in a highly competitive market. In order to remain competitive, the company's senior directors must have ready access to data needed to inform market-based decision-making. The company's directors have come up with the following set of questions to answer:

- Which models of guitar are most popular? Least popular?

- Which options and customizations are most popular? Least popular?

- Which models, options, and customizations are mentioned most favorably in product reviews and musician blogs? Which are mentioned least favorably?

- Which models, options, and customizations are most expensive to produce? Least expensive to produce?

- Which models, options, and customizations require the most and least manufacture time, labor hours, and process steps?

- Which models, options, and customizations return the most and least profit to the company?

- What features, as mentioned in product reviews and musician blogs, should be added to the company's offerings? What currently-offered features need to be improved?

Note that the answers to each of these questions will vary by geographic location and market segment. What sells well to a teenager in Singapore is different from what sells well to a concert guitarist in Stockholm.

What the company's directors want to determine (for each of the company's divisions, sales regions, and market segments) are the models, options, and customizations that should be promoted, and the ones that should be deprecated. Some types of options and customizations may not return enough profit to be worth offering. Others might need to be retained, but should be priced sufficiently to ensure a profit. It doesn't make sense to price two different options at $100 each if one takes 4 hours to assemble and the other takes 10 hours.

The company's directors also need to track market trends: the features and capabilities that currently excite and engage guitar players, and those that guitar players wish for and don't currently have. What's the next new thing, and can we identify it soon enough to beat our competitors to market with it?

Unfortunately, Blue Moon's data is dispersed across a wide variety of data platforms, including an aging mainframe whose data is virtually inaccessible to everyone except a few in IT, and a host of distributed SQL databases. Company workers have developed, at enormous time and expense, a plethora of Microsoft Access databases and Excel spreadsheets with disparate sets of data maintained by various individuals and departments. In one memorable instance, end-of-month reporting in one department is done by merging the contents of six different Access databases into a seventh![58]

The company's directors, having decided on the questions they need to answer, now need to work with their IT people to determine how to get the data they need. They also have to decide how to best turn that data into the information and insight they need to make decisions (data visualization and analytics). Furthermore, they have to address the question of how to validate the correctness of the data (data quality) and how to administer or oversee the content of the data in a way that ensures its continual availability and value to the business (data governance). They start by dividing the data requirements into three general categories.

DATA WE HAVE (AND CAN GET EASILY)

This includes data that currently resides in the company's application databases, including the mainframe. Access to the company's data on the various platforms could be obtained using a data virtualization product; however, since the company's application portfolio is badly in need of updating, the company's directors make a strategic decision: existing application data will be migrated and integrated into an Operational Data Store (ODS) on a data appliance.

Existing applications will either be rewritten to use the ODS as a data source (possibly using a standard set of web services for data transport) or replaced by Cloud-based vendor applications (which also will use web services to transport data to and from the ODS). The existing databases and data platforms will be deprecated. This strategy will give the company a single data repository that can support applications, web services, and BI, while enabling it to reduce the operational costs associated with maintaining multiple data platforms and stores of data.

---

[58] I'm fudging the truth a little here. It was actually 13 Access databases. No, I'm not kidding.

Note that this is a different architecture (and a different strategy) from a data warehouse, a data vault, or an implementation of Hadoop. In these architectures, data is stored and then provisioned in support of BI and analytics applications, whereas the ODS will support day-to-day operational needs as well as BI. It's the difference between having to go to a bank and withdraw cash from a safe deposit box and being able to carry a debit card with you wherever you go!

Data extracted from Blue Moon's various application databases includes Order, Product, Option, and Customer data. Sales forecasts are loaded from an Access database in the marketing department.

DATA WE DON'T HAVE (BUT CAN GET EASILY)

This includes data that can be obtained from a third party, including sales figures for various brands and models of guitars; a quarterly summary of this data is purchased from an outside "data aggregation" firm. This data supports the company's sales and marketing efforts, and will now be added to the new ODS.

Another set of needed data identified by Blue Moon's directors is time-and-motion data related to the manufacturing process. For each model of guitar, and each option that is available on that model, we want to know how long it takes to assemble, and how many process steps are involved. This enables us to determine the total labor cost of each model and option; it also gives us a base of data that can be used to identify process changes that can improve efficiency and lower costs while reducing manufacturing defects.[59]

An outside consulting firm is hired to begin the work of observing (and videotaping) the manufacturing process, tabulating the results, and entering the data into the ODS.

---

[59] Cognizant readers will recognize this as the Lean Six Sigma approach to quality management and process improvement.

DATA WE DON'T HAVE (AND CAN'T GET EASILY)

As noted above, the company would very much like to "mine" social media data, in order to determine how Blue Moon's products and services compare to those of its competitors. They would also like to direct the company's product development and marketing efforts based on sentiment from social media, including product reviews (including reviews of its competitors' products) and content from musicians' blogs.

Blue Moon does not have the technology or knowledge to accomplish this. After discussion with IT management, the company directors decide to partner with one or more Cloud-based big data providers on some proof of concept projects. After sending out RFIs (Requests for Information) to a small group of companies, they select two potential partners and do one POC with each: a sentiment analysis of Blue Moon products compared with competitor products, and a sentiment analysis of guitar features (existing features preferred by guitar players, non-existing features desired by guitar players, and existing features not preferred by guitar players).

After the POCs have been successfully completed, Blue Moon will choose one of the companies to partner with, and will have that company perform social media sentiment analysis on a quarterly basis. The results of those analyses will be put into structured form and loaded into the ODS to be used for further analysis, visualization, and decision-making.

DESIGNING THE SOLUTION

Blue Moon's directors have completed their assessment of the company's BI needs; they now have an understanding of the questions they need answers to, and the data that will provide those answers. The next step of the process involves working with the company's IT architects (including its data, BI, and application architects) to design an appropriate solution.

As mentioned above, concerns about the quality of the data in Blue Moon's aging mainframe systems, along with a desire to upgrade Blue Moon's application portfolio to include Cloud-based and SOA-based applications (and retire the old applications and databases), has led Blue Moon to take an ODS-based approach. Data from multiple application databases and other sources will be integrated into the ODS in a form that expedites BI delivery while enabling support for Blue Moon's new portfolio of applications.

This means that Blue Moon will have to make use of the Pattern-based approach to BI described in this book: in order to achieve short-term BI objectives, data from source systems will have to be "forklifted" into tables in the ODS and covered with information views. As the ODS is designed and built out, those views will be repointed to the ODS tables, and additional views needed to support applications will be built.

ACQUIRING THE DATA

Blue Moon has now completed the first iteration(s) of what will be regarded as an ongoing (i.e. Agile) BI process:

1. Identify a problem to be solved, a question to be answered, or a capability to be achieved.
2. Identify the data needed to achieve the desired goal.
3. Identify the source(s) of the data, and assess the difficulty involved in obtaining it.
4. Put a process in place to acquire that data from the most reliable source(s).

For each set of data that's been identified as needed, a process (hopefully an Agile one) must be put into place to acquire and store this data, along with its associated metadata. The technology used will vary based on an organization's target state BI architecture, IT culture, vendor relationships, and budget. However, the steps involved will usually look something like this:

5. Profile the data.

6. Model the data.
7. Design and build the data structures.
8. Extract the data from the source, transform and cleanse it as necessary, and load it into the data store.
9. Document and publish the metadata for this data.

It is this part of the BI delivery process that is fraught with both error and inefficiency, and thus needs to be improved, iteratively and over time, using Agile methodologies. At first, this process will be mostly manual, using whatever tools are readily available, for the purpose of getting useable data to the business as quickly as possible.

Data may be profiled using queries against a database, or even visually. If a quality data modeling tool isn't available, data design may need to be done on a white board, or using a developer tool such as Microsoft's Visual Studio. ETL may be completed using hand-coded programs (such as COBOL programs on the mainframe), database stored procedures, or a scripting language such as Windows PowerShell. Metadata may be captured and published on a spreadsheet.

Over time, as inefficiencies and bottlenecks in this process become apparent, concerted efforts will be made to improve them, replacing manual processes with automated ones and giving BI developers better and faster tools to work with. When Blue Moon commits to BI, it must also commit to the process of improving BI delivery, which means dedicating resources and spending money.

The important thing is to commit to the process of delivering value (in the form of actionable data) to the business as quickly and effectively as possible, identifying the problems and bottlenecks, and working iteratively (and collaboratively) to improve the delivery process over time.

It is also necessary to understand why each step of the process is important, in order to maximize the value delivered from each step, and to create a process that makes sense for the chosen BI architecture. If the data is being stored in a relational database, for example, it makes sense to profile and model the data before creating the schema and storing the data (to reduce ETL problems caused by data anomalies). This initial data profiling and modeling makes sense even if your target database is a NoSQL data store.[60] However, if you're moving your data into Hadoop, it probably makes more sense to load the data first and then profile it.

Profile data to the extent needed to identify the characteristics of the data and its possible range of values, and to reduce uncertainty about what business data is represented by a particular data field. Model data to the extent needed to give all BI stakeholders a common shared understanding of the data, to ensure that data is stored in a form that allows it to be easily consumed, extended, integrated, and reused. Document and publish metadata in a form that answers the most commonly asked questions about the data, and reduces uncertainty about how best to use it.

Above all, don't focus on perfection; keep the focus on delivering value continuously and incrementally, and improving delivery over time.

PROVISIONING THE DATA

Blue Moon's business directors and IT architects have now addressed the work of defining the BI "opportunity space," identifying the data needed to drive BI value, designing the BI infrastructure, and acquiring the data. Getting the data into the data store (on whatever platform, in whatever form) is the first half of the BI delivery process. The second half is getting the data out of the data store into the hands of business users in a useable form. The steps involved are as follows:

10. Create a virtual representation of the data in a semantic form that users are comfortable working with.

---

[60] See, for example, Steve Hoberman's excellent book *Data Modeling for MongoDB* (Technics Publications LLC, 2014).

11. Give users access to BI tools that let them work with this data in an intuitive way.
12. Give users access to metadata that answers their questions and addresses their concerns about the data.
13. Give users the ability to share and publish the results of their analyses across the organization, and consume data created by others.

Again, part of this process may start out being more manual and "low tech." Data may be virtualized by creating information views in the database or data store, and restricting data access to these views rather than the underlying database tables. This gives users a more business-friendly and meaningful representation of the data, reduces or eliminates the need to code semantic meaning into the data store, and helps insulate business users from changes in the database schema.

Metadata can be shared via SharePoint or some similar document repository, or even stored in tables in the data store and made available for querying through a view or views. At some later point, the organization can explore options for automating some of these processes, through the use of data virtualization portals and metadata repositories.

What mustn't be skimped on are the end-user data visualization and analytics tools. In order for a BI initiative to succeed, business users must have tools that work well for them, and that they are comfortable with (and enthusiastic about) using. Make sure your users have the tools they need and will use from the get-go.

MANAGING THE DATA

Blue Moon has now successfully deployed several iterations of data into its ODS and delivered significant value into the hands of its business users. Changes and enhancements to the business include:

- A redesigned website instantly directs customers to the nearest guitar shop that stocks the instrument they are looking for. If no shop has this particular instrument, the search will direct the customer to the shop closest to a Blue Moon distributor that has the instrument in stock.

- Models and options that are not generating significant revenue have been identified and removed from Blue Moon's catalog. Discount offers on existing instruments have been made available to Blue Moon's preferred customers, in order to remove these instruments from inventory.

- Remaining models and options have been repriced based on the cost of manufacture, to ensure that Blue Moon isn't losing money on these instruments.

- Customer demand for particular models and options has been analyzed, and stock at Blue Moon's distribution warehouses has been adjusted to ensure that instruments with the highest demand in a given geographical area are immediately available from the warehouse in that area.

- Blue Moon is now able to work more effectively with retailers in a given area to ensure that the instruments they stock more accurately reflect customer demand in that area.

- Blue Moon's business analysts and marketers now have immediate access to data needed for visualizations and reports; they no longer have to wait days, weeks, or even months for data to be extracted from the mainframe and provisioned in an Access database. Furthermore, with this load removed from the mainframe, performance of Blue Moon's day-to-day transactional systems has improved measurably, and system downtime has been reduced.

However, as Blue Moon's business people work with the data, some problems begin to surface. It is discovered, for example, that there is no consistent denoting of part numbers; the same part may have different part numbers depending on which division purchased it, and from which supplier. This makes it difficult to determine which instruments that part is used on, and what the failure rate of that part is per model. Also, labor codes used in manufacturing are not consistent across Blue Moon's divisions; this makes it difficult to accurately gauge costs, set prices, and improve processes across the company.

Some data anomalies have been identified. For example, an examination of shipment data has uncovered duplicate shipment records, as well as orphaned shipment transaction data with no associated shipment records!

There are also disagreements about the business meaning of particular data items; take, for example, "shipment date." Does this refer to the date the instrument leaves the factory, the date it's sent to the retailer, or the date it's delivered to the customer?

Blue Moon begins the process of creating a Data Governance Competency Center within its organization. A representative from each division and business unit (accounting, manufacturing, sales, etc.) is selected, based on experience and familiarity with that part of the business and its data. These designated "data stewards" meet once a month to discuss and resolve data issues.

Decisions are made and published on Blue Moon's data governance SharePoint site, which gives business users access to the metadata catalog and a link that they can use to report any data problems, issues, or questions to the data governance committee. The committee has the authority to dictate changes in business processes and/or IT systems in order to resolve problems and issues that have been identified. Some of these changes may necessitate changes to the BI data store, ETL processes, information views, etc.

Over time, additional initiatives begin to emerge under the direction of the data governance committee. Data stewards who have received Lean or Six Sigma training begin executing data quality projects to identify data problems and get them fixed, both in the BI data store and in the source systems. The business impact of bad data, and the business benefits of good data, start to be quantitatively measured. Rather than trying to create perfect data across the entire organization, resources are directed to those areas in which improvements in data quality will produce the most measureable business benefits.

Master data management (MDM) programs are also created, so that master data (e.g. product and part data) maintained in the BI data store can be published back into transactional systems (and databases); this helps ensure that Blue Moon's day-to-day operations are using the most accurate data.

MANAGING THE BI PROCESS

Finally, Blue Moon's directors face the question of managing and improving the BI delivery process itself. Using an approach similar to the data governance model described above, Blue Moon creates a BI Competency Center, consisting of representatives from both the business and IT. They meet once a month to discuss new BI capabilities that should be created, business opportunities that should be pursued, problems that must be resolved, inefficiencies and bottlenecks that should be eliminated, improvements that can be made, new data sources that should be acquired, and new technology that should be explored.

Lean and Six Sigma Belts are given the task of identifying inefficiencies in the BI delivery process and improving them. Proofs of concept (POCs) are created for new tools and technologies that can improve Blue Moon's BI capabilities. In particular, the company wants to analyze manufacturing data in real time to identify manufacturing and process defects during the manufacturing process, so that problems can be fixed before the instrument is completely assembled and ready for final inspection. Tools that help streamline some of the more burdensome parts of the BI delivery process (e.g. ETL, data design) are evaluated and purchased.

The goal of the BI Competency Center (BICC) is to ensure that each successive BI project delivers increasing value at lower cost, and that the cost of maintaining Blue Moon's BI infrastructure does not exceed the value it produces for the company. Indeed, the BICC's goal is to see a year-by-year decrease in maintenance costs for its BI infrastructure, and a year-by-year increase in the business value it delivers.

As you might imagine, this is not a short or an easy journey. But with a dedicated focus on value delivery and continuous improvement, Blue Moon is assured that its nascent BI efforts will pay dividends to the company for years to come.

Key Points

- The BI delivery process implemented by Blue Moon consists of the following steps:

  A. Identify the Data.
  B. Design the Solution.
  C. Acquire the Data.
  D. Provision the Data.
  E. Manage the Data.
  F. Manage the BI Process.

- Data sources are identified and acquired based on their importance to the business and the ease with which the data can be acquired.

- Processes start out as manual, inefficient, and "low tech." Over time, processes are improved and automated, and more effective tooling is acquired as its value can be demonstrated to the business.

- The organization grows in BI maturity over time. Issues of data governance and BI process management are identified and processes are put in place to improve the company in these areas.

- Emphasis is placed on: 1) delivering value to the business, 2) continually improving the BI delivery process, 3) improving the quality of data delivered to the business, and 4) reducing the cost of maintaining the BI infrastructure.

- Lean, Six Sigma, and Agile methodologies can be used effectively to continually improve both the quality and effectiveness of BI delivery.

- Data governance and BI Competency Centers provide effective means for the business and IT to work together to improve the company's ability to manage its data and information assets.

Afterword

I wish I could write more, for much more needs to be written. However, my vacation is over, and I hear the call of my publisher saying it's time to put the book to bed. So we'll have to regard this work as one more in a continuing series of conversations, too brief and too imperfect, but part of the eternal thread of thought and feeling that binds us all together. As historian Harry Golden has said, "we are all on a single ball of twine, and every few yards or so we meet."

Later in that same essay, he writes: "the whole of civilization really revolves around *us*—each of us individually."

If reading this book has accomplished nothing else, I hope it has made you think a bit about the garden you wish to be in, and what it would feel like to walk around in it, and what steps you might take to find it. The principal cause of failure, I have always thought, is failure of imagination. You have to see yourself in the place you want to be, before you can even start thinking about how to make the journey there.

BI initiatives, like gardening, are a lot of work, but the rewards are many. And, as has been said, if life was meant to be easy, we'd plant weeds in our gardens instead of flowers.

As always, I wish you continuing success on your journey.

Larry Burns has worked in IT for more than 30 years as a database developer, DBA, data modeler, application developer, consultant, and teacher. He holds a B.S. in Mathematics from the University of Washington, and a Master's degree in Software Engineering from Seattle University. He currently works for a global Fortune 500 company as a Data and BI Architect and Data Engineer (i.e., data modeler).

He contributed material on Database Development and Database Operations Management to the first edition of DAMA International's Data Management Body of Knowledge (DAMA-DMBOK), and is a former instructor and advisor in the certificate program for Data Resource Management at the University of Washington in Seattle. He has written numerous articles for TDAN.com and DMReview.com, and is the author of *Building the Agile Database* (Technics Publications LLC, 2011).

His interests include music, gardening, and landscaping. He is also an active member of Toastmasters, the international public speaking organization.

He lives in Kent, Washington with his wife Becky.

Agile Alliance. A wealth of information about Agile development, its philosophy, and best practices can be found on the website of the Agile Alliance at http://www.agilealliance.org/.

Agile Data. Information about traditional approaches to Agile data development can be found at http://www.agiledata.org/.

Ann Lovejoy. Ann's seminal book on Sustainable Gardening, from which this book derives its inspiration, is *The Ann Lovejoy Handbook of Northwest Gardening* (Sasquatch Books, Seattle WA, 2003, http://www.sasquatchbooks.com). This book is well worth reading, even if you don't live in the Pacific Northwest!

DAMA International. DAMA International is the recognized source for education, certification, and information regarding best practices in the data management profession. Information about DAMA can be found on their website at http://www.dama.org/.

DAMA DMBOK. DAMA International's Data Management Body of Knowledge (DMBOK) is a compendium of standards and industry best practices for the management of data as an enterprise asset. Copies of the DMBOK (in print, PDF, or CD-ROM) can be obtained from Technics Publications at http://bit.ly/2aAVwx6.

Data Governance. There are three common approaches to data governance. The approach advocated by James Orr in his book *Data Governance for the Executive* (Senna Publishing LLC, 2011) promotes the creation of an enterprise-wide DG organization separate from existing business units. The "Non-Invasive" approach advocated by Robert Seiner in his book *Non-Invasive Data Governance* (Technics Publications LLC, 2014) implements DG within existing business units and with current staff. The approach advocated by John Ladley in his book *Data Governance* (Elsevier/Morgan Kaufmann, 2012) promotes a middle ground: creation of a separate DG structure that eventually subsumes into existing business units and business processes. All are valuable books, and I recommend reading all of them.

EIM (Enterprise Information Management). This term refers to the collection of best practices for effectively managing data assets across an enterprise or organization. Information about EIM can be found on the website of the EIM Institute at http://www.eiminstitute.org/.

Lean Thinking. Often (erroneously) described as "Lean Manufacturing," the Lean approach focuses on continually increasing customer value delivery while decreasing waste and inefficiency. Information about Lean principles can be found on the website of the Lean Enterprise Institute at http://www.lean.org, as well as in the book *Lean Thinking* by James P. Womack and Daniel T. Jones.

Master data management. As with Data Governance, there are a number of possible approaches to MDM. A good reference work to start with is David Loshin's book *Master Data Management* (Elsevier/Morgan Kaufmann, 2009).

Non-invasive data governance. An approach to data governance that leverages the existing data management efforts of organizational workers and seeks to formalize and improve these efforts (rather than impose a new external data governance structure). Information about this approach can be found on Robert Seiner's websites at http://www.kikconsulting.com and http://www.tdan.com.

Six Sigma. The Six Sigma methodology focuses on improving processes by reducing or eliminating process variability. It differs from the Lean approach by focusing on improving existing processes rather than increasing value delivery, and on reducing defects rather than reducing waste and inefficiency. However, the two approaches are often combined into a single approach often referred to as **Lean Six Sigma**. Information about Six Sigma can be found at http://www.esixsigma.org/and http://www.asq.org.

AD   Agile Development

Agile   An iterative approach to application (software) development, based on early and continuous delivery of working software.

Attribute   A characteristic or property of an Entity in a logical data model.

BI   Business intelligence; the analysis and reporting of data in a way that allows the business to improve processes, create and strengthen stakeholder relationships, and recognize and take advantage of new and changing market conditions.

BDUF   Big design up front; creation of a large number of analysis and design artifacts at the beginning of a development project, before any actual coding begins.

CEP   Complex Event Processing; the use of real-time (streaming) data analytics to determine the appropriate response to system events as they occur.

CRM   Customer Relationship Management; the process of understanding and improving a company's relationships with its customer stakeholders.

DAMA   The Data Administration Management Association; the international organization for data management professionals.

Dashboard   A graphical representation of integrated and distilled data that allows business users to interact in a meaningful way with the metrics of their organization.

Data Mart	An integrated store of data that supports BI and analytics processes. Data marts are departmental in scope and reflect a single business subject area. Data is conformed to a dimensional schema and is pre-aggregated for improved performance.
Data Vault	An integrated store of data that supports BI and analytics processes. Data vaults store raw data values in a hyper-normalized form that allows changes in data values over time to be easily tracked.
Data Warehouse	An integrated store of data that supports BI and analytics processes. Data warehouses relate to the enterprise in scope, are historical (rather than real-time), conform to a defined schema (rather than containing raw data), and are normalized in structure (rather than aggregated).
DBA	Database Administrator; alternatively, Database Analyst.
DBMS	Database Management System; the software that enables users and applications to interact with databases.
DMBOK	The Data Management Body of Knowledge; a compendium of information and best practices in data and information management.
EDW	Enterprise Data Warehouse. See "Data Warehouse".
EIM	Enterprise Information Management; the collection of best practices for effectively managing data assets across an enterprise or organization.
Entity	A business object (such as Customer or Product), as represented in a logical data model.

ESB   Enterprise Service Bus; software that controls the routing of messages between web services in a Service-Oriented Architecture (see SOA).

Hadoop   Java-based software that supports the distributed processing and analysis of very large data sets across multiple processing nodes.

IT   Information Technology. The principal job of an IT organization is to facilitate, improve, and sustain enterprise-wide data and information processes.

KPI   Key Performance Indicator; a standard or goal against which organizational performance metrics are measured.

Metric   A measurement of organizational performance.

Metadata   Information about the characteristic properties of a data object or structure, usually contained within that object or structure. As used in this book, it also refers to information needed to help a business user assess the potential value or risk of a given set of data.

NoSQL   A data storage and processing solution not based on relational database technology. Relational databases are based on the concept of "schema on write": data must be predefined before it can be stored. NoSQL databases are based on the concept of "schema on read": data can be stored without being predefined, but is put into a defined form at the time it is retrieved.

OLAP   Online Analytical Processing; a technique for analyzing data by structuring it in the form of a multi-dimensional "cube," from which two-dimensional "slices" can be cut.

OLTP   Online Transactional Processing; the day-to-day operational processes of an IT organization.

POC   Proof of Concept; a small-scale implementation of a new technology or business capability, intended to identify the most workable approach or solution to a given problem.

RDBMS   Relational Database Management System; software that supports the creation and use of relational databases.

Refactor   To improve an application or database object without changing its behavior.

ROI   Return on Investment; what IT and BI expenditures are supposed to deliver and oftentimes don't.

SOA   Service-Oriented Architecture; an architecture that allows applications and databases to interact through the medium of a web services "hub," rather than communicating directly.

Sprint   In the Scrum approach to Agile, one iteration of a development project.

SQL   Structured Query Language; used to create objects and to query and manipulate data in relational databases.

SME   Subject matter expert; a business or IT person with advanced knowledge of a particular application or business process.

TCO   Total Cost of Ownership; the sum total of initial investment, development, and maintenance over time for an IT application or database. This should never exceed the value it provides to the organization.

XML   Extensible Markup Language; a way of transmitting and/or storing data in text form.

Index